Introducing Leadership

Introducing Leadership

David Pardey

ELSEVIER

AMSTERDAM • BOSTON • HEIDELBERG • LONDON • NEW YORK • OXFORD
PARIS • SAN DIEGO • SAN FRANCISCO • SINGAPORE • SYDNEY • TOKYO
Butterworth-Heinemann is an imprint of Elsevier

Butterworth-Heinemann is an imprint of Elsevier
Linacre House, Jordan Hill, Oxford OX2 8DP, UK
30 Corporate Drive, Suite 400, Burlington, MA 01803, USA

First edition 2007

Notice
No responsibility is assumed by the publisher for any injury and/or damage
to persons or property as a matter of products liability, negligence or
otherwise, or from any use or operation of any methods, products, instructions
or ideas contained in the material herein. Because of rapid advances in the
medical sciences, in particular, independent verification of diagnoses and drug
dosages should be made

British Library Cataloguing in Publication Data
A catalogue record for this book is available from the British Library

Library of Congress Cataloging-in-Publication Data
A catalog record for this book is available from the Library of Congress

ISBN-13: 978-0-7506-6901-6
ISBN-10: 0-7506-6901-2

For information on all Butterworth-Heinemann publications
visit our web site at http://books.elsevier.com

Typeset by Charon Tec Ltd, Chennai, India
www.charontec.com

Printed and bound in the United Kingdom

06 07 08 09 10   10 9 8 7 6 5 4 3 2 1

Working together to grow
libraries in developing countries

www.elsevier.com | www.bookaid.org | www.sabre.org

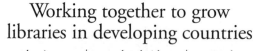

Contents

CONTENTS

CONTENTS

CONTENTS

CONTENTS

Figures

Introduction

What images do the words 'leader' and 'manager' conjure up in your mind? Do you see leaders as heroic figures, leading underdogs to victory in a David and Goliath-style battle, like Ernest Shackleton bringing back his crew safely from the Antarctic or Steve Jobs leading Apple in its seemingly one-sided battle with the ubiquitous Microsoft Windows?

In 1914, Shackleton led an expedition to Antarctica on board the Endurance. For more than a year they were all stranded, watching their vessel crushed by the ice. They then escaped across the South Atlantic wastes in the remaining three lifeboats to make landfall on a deserted rock. From here Shackleton and five men sailed a further 800 miles to South Georgia and then walked across a frozen mountain range to reach a whaling station. Finally, Shackleton led the rescuers back for his men, bringing them all safely home[1].

Steve Jobs founded Apple in 1971 (with Steve Wozniak) and, 13 years later, launched the Apple Mac, the first PC with a 'graphical user interface', predating the Microsoft Windows GUI by a year. But, in 1985, Jobs was forced out of the company he had created, only to rejoin the nearly bankrupt Apple (as iCEO or interim chief executive) 11 years later and save it with the launch of the iMac, the iPod and iTunes. Jobs has a reputation for being difficult to work with yet also as a visionary. He was responsible for turning the GUI into the norm for computing; it was during his lengthy exile from Apple that he founded NeXt, the hardware on which Tim Berners-Lee created the work-wide web; and he also still heads Pixar (the producers of computer animated films such as *Toy Story* and *Finding Nemo*).

Are leaders people who are slightly larger than life, then; driven, charismatic, inspirational, far-sighted, essential when things are getting tough but an optional extra in a smooth-running operation? And what about managers? Are they bureaucrats, administrators, budget-holders, and performance monitors, who sit in offices watching those who do the work, forever dreaming up ways of

1

making life more difficult? Or are they essential for creating the smooth-running, successful organizations that most people would like to work for? Steve Jobs is very much the driven leader, inspirational yet, at the same time, difficult to work with, constantly striving to achieve his vision for the future and unwilling to compromise in the process. The same could be said about Shackleton, yet it was his careful planning and minute attention to detail that ensured that his men all survived, despite tremendous hardships. Was it his leadership ability that prevented disaster, or was it his managerial abilities? Or was it both?

Introducing Leadership is not about famous explorers or corporate CEOs – in fact, they are rarely mentioned – but all about the everyday leadership by first line and middle managers[2] of people working in their organizations. Its emphasis is severely practical because it starts from the assumption that leadership is based on skills and behaviours that most people can acquire, and that most of the people working in organizations want effective leadership from the people who manage them on a day-to-day basis.

If you run a company, civil service department or charity this book is not for you – there are plenty of books out there about leadership at the top of organizations. However, it is for all the hard-pressed managers in your organization who have to motivate and inspire the people who perform the tasks that make the organization function on a day-to-day basis.

The 13 chapters in *Introducing Leadership* are loosely grouped around three themes. The first, covering Chapters 1 to 5, looks at the nature of leadership and the characteristics and skills needed to perform this role effectively, finishing up in Chapter 5 by looking at how you can develop these characteristics and skills yourself. The second theme, in Chapters 6 to 9, looks at some of the practicalities of leadership in dealing with people. It starts by examining how organization structures and people's roles and responsibilities affect behaviour, goes on to look at the implications of leading individuals and groups or teams, and finishes by examining how leaders handle conflict. The third and final theme, in Chapters 10 to 13, looks at the role of leadership in crisis, and in bringing about improvement, innovation and change.

In a fast-moving, ever-changing social and economic environment, organizations and the people who work in them need effective leadership at all levels. *Introducing Leadership* is written specifically to help people who are committed to becoming more effective leaders to achieve their goals. It is also designed to demystify leadership and show that, in practice, nearly all of us have the ability to become effective leaders if we have the commitment and know how to it. If you have that commitment, why not let *Introducing Leadership* help you find out how?

Notes

1 There is a very interesting account of Shackleton's trip to the Antarctic and a discussion of his leadership approach in *Shackleton's Way* by Margot Morrell and Stephanie Capparell.
2 The terms 'first line manager' and 'middle manager' are used frequently throughout *Introducing Leadership*. There is a brief definition of these two terms and of 'team leader' at the end of the book.

1 Being a leader

In this chapter you will get a chance to explore what is meant by the words 'leadership' and 'management' and how the two fit together. A lot has been written about both over the last century or so, not all of it particularly innovative – often the same ideas reappear in slightly different words. However, there are some common themes that clearly emerge and these provide the basis for agreeing a commonsense definition of what it is that leaders do.

Leadership or management?

It is worth going back to basics to get some insights into what leaders and managers are, and what their role is. Back at the turn of the 20th century, Henri Fayol, a French engineer and management theorist laid the grounds for what is often called the 'classical' management tradition – in fact, he was very much one of its founders. Like Frederick Taylor (who helped Henry Ford invent mass production in his Highland Park car factory in 1913), he saw management as being very task focused, about using resources as efficiently as possible.

Fayol's five key functions of management are still widely used today to define the role, seeing management as being to:

1 plan (and look ahead)
2 organize
3 command
4 coordinate
5 control (inspect and provide feedback).

If you were to draw up a list of all the tasks that you and others normally perform as managers you would find that most, if not all, could be fitted into these five functional areas. Whether this helps us or not, is another matter. It could be that Fayol had recognized exactly what management is about, or that he has identified five

1 Specialization and division of labour	9 Chain/line of authority
2 Authority with responsibility	10 Order
3 Discipline	11 Equity
4 Unity of command	12 Lifetime jobs (for good workers)
5 Unity of direction	13 Initiative
6 Subordination of individual interest to the group interest	14 *Esprit de corps* (literally 'the spirit of the body', meaning subscribing to the values, standards and culture of the group of which you are part)
7 Remuneration	
8 Centralization	

Figure 1.1   Fayol's 14 principles of management

categories that are so broad that more or less anything would fit into them! However, underpinning these five functions are 14 principles (Figure 1.1), principles that give a fuller picture of Fayol's view of the role.

These principles emphasize a fairly strong 'command and control' philosophy of management, but tempered by such 20th century concepts as 'lifetime jobs' and 21st century concepts as 'equity'. If you were to draw up a similar list of leadership principles, it is doubtful if most of these qualities would appear. We probably would not expect specialization and division of labour, discipline or remuneration to be included in such a list, although we might expect concepts such as authority with responsibility, unity of direction, initiative and *esprit de corps* to be included.

Why go into such detail about someone long dead and buried, when there are so many more recent contributors to our understanding of leadership (and management)? Because what Fayol was writing over 100 years ago could still be written today, with some of the principles of management being just as relevant to our perception of what leadership is, while others being clearly only appropriate to a definition of management. This is, because management and leadership are inextricably linked, but different. The best way to make sense of what leadership is, is to appreciate both the linkages (and overlaps) between the two, and their differences.

Exploring the linkages

The interrelationship between management and leadership has always been difficult to disentangle. Some 60 years after Fayol had published his key work (*Administration Industrielle et Générale*) in 1916, Lawrence Appley came up with a definition of management that could just as easily be (and frequently is) thought of as a definition of leadership. Appley was a leading member of the American Management Association and, in his influential book *Formula For Success: A core concept of management*, published in 1974, he presented leadership as a quality that he expected managers to possess. Appley described management as 'getting things done through other people', an easy definition to remember, but one that does present problems. Where do budgeting, quality assurance or risk assessment fit into this definition? – all important functional responsibilities of managers, but not easily described as 'getting things done through other people' (although fitting well into Fayol's description of the management role). However, the definition also works well as a description of leadership, and it is one we will return to later.

This confusion between 'leadership' and 'management' – or at least, the difficulty of distinguishing between the two – is partly due to the way that the labels have evolved in their meaning over time. The size and organization of businesses and public sector bodies changed so much during the 20th century that what managers and leaders were, and what they did, was transformed. It is worth remembering that, until the late 1960s, it was very uncommon for the word leader or manager to be used at all in respect of the public sector, and only the more senior employees of private sector organizations would be called managers. Nowadays, we recognize that managerial and leadership roles and responsibilities are present far more widely and one consequence has been a greater emphasis on trying to define what these different roles actually entail. In the process, we have had to try to agree just what the words 'manager' and 'leader' mean.

Are you a leader or a manager?

Whatever our personal view of leaders and leadership, most of us would far rather be called a good leader than a great manager. The images conjured up by the labels 'manager' and 'leader' are essentially stereotypes and far too simplistic as descriptions of the roles, let alone definitions of the terms, but both have a grain of truth. Managers are often thought of as bureaucrats, administrators, budget-holders, performance monitors, and leaders as heroic, slightly larger than life, charismatic, inspirational, far-sighted figures, but reverse the two labels and it is just plain silly.

Leadership is a much more positive label, slightly mythic, what Americans call a 'motherhood and apple pie' concept – no one could possibly oppose leadership. On the other hand, management does not always get such a good press. At best, managers are seen as a necessary evil, adding little to the sum of human goodness, but somewhat parasitical, feeding off the work of others. Time and again the health service is criticized for having too many managers and not enough nurses and doctors; the BBC under Director-General John Birt was pilloried for the way resources were seen to be diverted to over-burdensome management structures, and Birt himself was parodied as a Dalek using management speak rather than real language.

This is a book about leadership so surely it supports that view, doesn't it? Putting the case for leadership rather than management, showing how leadership is the solution to the management problem. In one word, no! Throughout this book you will find that leadership is presented as the counterpart to management, rather as 'heads' is the counterpart to 'tails' on a coin. You cannot have a proper coin without both and you cannot say one side is more important, more necessary or better than the other.

Each face of the coin exists in part because the other face exists. Leadership will be presented as the counterpart to management, no better, no worse. In fact, one argument that *Introducing Leadership* will be putting very forcibly is that effective leaders have to be effective managers, and vice versa. They are not alternatives you can choose between, heads or tails. They are different but equal, and equally vital in the modern organizational environment.

In this chapter you will have a chance to explore just what is meant by 'leadership' (and 'management', to explore the differences and interrelationships) and why it is such a critical part of the management role, especially for first line and middle managers. Subsequent chapters in this first Section of *Introducing Leadership* will explore the skills, practices and behaviours that you need to develop to be an effective leader. Section 2 will focus on the leadership of people, and some of the opportunities and challenges that leaders face in getting the best out of the people they lead, and Section 3 on the role and practice of leadership in bringing about innovation and change. But before that, let us go back to the beginning and ask the question, just what is this thing called leadership?

What is leadership?

Leadership is a bit like 'good art' – we may have difficulty in defining it, but we know it when we see it (or experience it). And, although that may not seem very helpful, it is quite significant, because it tells us something about leadership, something that probably is not true of management. Leadership is something that people see or experience, personally. It is above all about the relationship between the leader and those people being led. A leader without followers is about as meaningful as a bicycle without wheels – it may possess most of the necessary components but without wheels it cannot do the one thing it is intended to do.

A leader without followers may be as useless as a bike without wheels, but the problem cannot be so easily resolved. It is easy enough to fit wheels to a bike (at least, it is not too difficult), but you cannot fit followers to a leader. Leaders have to create their own followers, and that is probably the most significant characteristic of leaders, that they can create followers. As a definition it does not get us very far ('leaders are people who have followers') but it does point us in the right direction. There are managers in charge of money (financial managers), marketing (marketing managers), sales (sales managers), engineering (engineering managers) and so on, managers who may have responsibility for people but just as easily, may not. The five functions of management that Fayol first listed can just as easily be applied to inanimate (and even abstract) entities – creative managers in advertising agencies can plan, organize and coordinate creative activity. How well they can command or control it is debatable, but certainly they are managing something that only exists as an abstraction.

That is not true of leadership. Leaders need followers, and one definition of leadership is that leaders are people who *inspire others to follow*. This definition of leadership implies some degree of voluntarism in 'followership', that it is not enough for leaders to say 'I am going that way and you must follow' but they must be able to say 'I am going that way; will you follow me?' In the first case ('I am going that way and you must follow'), the compulsion to follow is what Fayol called 'command', a function of management, and most people in management and leadership positions will have to direct people from time to time. However, when people are being asked to put in the extra that is needed to get the job done well, or when are they are being asked to do something above and beyond their normal role and responsibility, it is then that leadership becomes essential. That is when people must choose to follow the route being set by the leader.

If followership is a characteristic of leadership, it still does not say what leadership is, any more than 'roundness' explains a wheel – it describes its most prominent characteristic. However, just as roundness is an essential feature of a wheel that leads towards defining what a wheel does, so followership points us towards a definition of leadership. A leader with followers must be going somewhere, and that means that they are moving or *changing* in some way, if only changing their location, and that they have some sense of *direction*. Without direction, a leader is aimless, and without movement, direction is useless because nobody can follow something that is not moving, no matter which way it is pointing (they are just queuing!).

This distinction between management and leadership, as two different but complementary roles, was most famously argued by John Kotter of Harvard Business School in an article he wrote for the Harvard Business Review, in 1990. In this article (*What leaders really do*) he described management as being about 'coping with complexity... (bringing) a degree of order and consistency to key dimensions like the quality and profitability of products'. In contrast, leadership 'is about coping with change'. To make this distinction clearer, Kotter compared three major aspects of the two roles (Figure 1.2).

Kotter's description of 'what managers do' is not too different from Fayol's, and his comparison with the role of leaders suggests that

---

What managers do
- Prepare plans and budgets, setting targets or goals for the future, to manage complexity
- Ensure the organization has the capacity to achieve the targets and goals by organizing (deciding on structures and roles) and staffing (filling those roles with the right people)
- Making sure that the plan is fulfilled by controlling what is done and solving problems

What leaders do
- Set a direction, develop a vision of where the organization should be going and the strategy for change to achieve that vision
- Aligning people to the direction being set, communicating it to people and building commitment to it
- Motivating and inspiring people so that they work to achieve the vision, drawing on their needs, values and emotions

---

Figure 1.2   Kotter's distinction between managers and leaders

the two roles are complementary rather than alternatives – effective organizations need both. For Kotter, the distinctive feature of the best organizations is that they get the balance between leadership and management right. He describes too many organizations as being 'over-managed and under-led'. He also places great emphasis on the growing significance of leadership because of the increasing rate of change, driven by new technology and increasing competition in a globalized economy.

Leadership, according to Kotter's definition, is about coping with change by giving direction and, as we will see later in this chapter, many of the distinctions that are made between leaders and managers, or between effective and ineffective leaders, focus on these two aspects. An organization that is not moving or changing is not developing, is static and unresponsive to the environment in which it operates – it lacks effective leadership. However, movement or change has no intrinsic value, it offers no benefits in itself. It is only movement or change that is for a purpose, is driven by a goal or a vision, has a clear sense of direction, that is valuable. Without that direction, the organization is probably better off staying where it is. Its people are just busy fools.

Doing the right thing

Another aspect of leadership that might help us to define it, or at least to understand it better, is the idea that leaders make decisions, particularly difficult decisions when there is great uncertainty or even danger, or when the choices they make are unpopular or that others are unwilling to make. Warren Bennis and Bert Nanus (in their book *Leaders: Their strategies for taking charge*) put it this way: 'Managers do things right and leaders are people who do the right thing'. This picks up on Fayol's idea of management, as being about getting things done properly (*doing it right*), and contrasts it with Kotter's idea of leadership as being about the purpose of that activity (*doing the right thing*).

Bennis and Nanus put forward four 'strategies' for doing the right thing:

1 Have a clear vision of where you want to go, and keep a clear focus on that vision

2 Communicate that vision to the people you lead so that it has real meaning for them, personally

11

3 Build real trust in your leadership through consistency in the way that you work

4 Have a strong belief in yourself and what you can do, while not ignoring your weaknesses.

From this you can see that their emphasis was very much on being fully aware of what you believe is the right thing to do, and following through on that 'vision' – that leadership is about having movement with direction and inspiring others to follow. By contrast, the idea that managers 'do things right' implies that the decisions have been made about what needs to be done and how it needs to be done. Their role is to make sure that the jobs are done in the way prescribed. This reflects Fayol's view of managers as people who:

1 *plan*, so that the resources that are needed are available, at the right time and in the right place

2 *organize* those resources so that they work in the most efficient and effective way

3 *command* people to perform their roles in the way that they should and prevent them from behaving in ways that endanger themselves and others

4 *coordinate* the resources so that they come together as planned to perform to the standards required

5 *control* resources, so that the products or services produced are what is wanted.

Without people taking responsibility for 'doing things right', nothing would get done. It might be the responsibility of an individual manager or it might be something shared among members of a (self-managing) team, but management is necessary.

What is right?

For Bennis and Nanus, the leader's role is to decide what managers and those they manage should be doing – that they are 'doing the right thing'. But 'right' can mean two things:

1 Doing what leads to a *desired result*, making decisions when outcomes are uncertain, when there is risk or even danger, the decision that produces the 'correct' result. So, when there is no risk or when outcomes are easily predictable despite which route you follow, then there is no great need for leadership, just simply making sure that the actions that are taken are done so as well as possible – good management.

2　Doing what is *ethically correct*, keeping to the set of values that are recognized as being appropriate in this situation. From this viewpoint, 'good' leaders do 'good' things, whereas people who follow courses of action that are morally doubtful or plain bad may be effective in achieving their goals but they cannot be called good leaders.

The idea of right as being what leads to the desired outcome follows from the idea of leadership as giving direction – a leader does not just set the direction but also makes the decisions about how best to get there. By thinking of leadership in this way we can get some idea of how leadership varies at different levels in organizations. Where there is the widest possible range of possible directions and great uncertainty how to achieve any one of them, which is usually at the head of the organization, then the demands on leaders are at their greatest. At other levels in the organization, the choice of direction may be more limited and the level of uncertainty less, but there is still a real need for leadership.

We will come back to this point many times in *Introducing Leadership*.

Reflection

Imagine you are flying in an aeroplane just coming into land. The airline you fly with encourages its personnel constantly to look for innovative solutions to problems, to seek to make continuous improvements to products and services, and always to aim to get things right first time. Which of these three principles (innovation, continuous improvement or right first time) do you want to be uppermost in the pilot's mind in preparing to land?

This example provides one way of thinking about leadership and management – doing the right thing and doing things right, both suggest that 'right first time' is the correct answer. But there will be times when the organization has to take risks in how it operates, introducing radical ways of working to survive in a competitive environment. Too great an emphasis on 'doing things right' may discourage innovation, but being innovative may well be the right thing to do – except when landing an aircraft, though!

Transformational leaders

The other meaning of 'right', as the morally right thing to do, is also something that we will look at in more detail in the next chapter, but it is important to raise it at this point because it is central to another theory of leadership that has become quite widely used. James MacGregor Burns, an American political scientist, developed a theory of leadership, which he described in his 1978 book *Leadership*. This was based on his belief that a moral dimension to behaviour was critical in determining its long-term effectiveness. He distinguished between two approaches to leadership that reflected the relationship between the leader and the led. Those he labelled *transactional leaders* are leaders who treat leadership as an exchange (a 'transaction') between leaders and followers. Thus, in his view, leaders who offered people power and economic prosperity in exchange for the right to lead them, like Hitler and Stalin, were engaged in a transaction (almost like a business deal).

By contrast, *transformational leaders* asked their followers to engage in an exchange of mutual trust and confidence, rather than material benefits, based on the quality of the relationship between them and their shared values and goals. Thus, in contrast to Hitler and Stalin, transformational leaders were people like Churchill ('I have nothing to offer but blood, sweat and tears') or, in a very different way, Mahatma Gandhi.

When applied in the arena of organizational management and leadership, the idea of transactional leadership tends all too easily to be equated with management, that management is about making sure that people put in a good day's work for a good day's pay (the transaction), whereas leadership is more inspirational, raising people's motivation to achieve more, better, by aligning their goals and values with that of the organization. In other words, encouraging people to achieve because they want to, not because they are being paid to. This is an interesting idea, and is another one that we will come back to, but its weakness is that it can be seen to treat management as a lesser (and morally dubious) role, compared to leadership.

For a start it could be taken to suggest that managers are Hitlers, leaders are Churchills! Burns himself said that 'divorced from ethics, leadership is reduced to management', suggesting that management is, by definition, some kind of moral-free zone. But what is wrong

14

with the idea that a transaction could be the basis for getting tasks completed, as well as people are able to do them, if that is what they are employed to do? The idea of a transaction is central to our understanding of employment (which is, after all, a contract) and any transaction is a two-way flow of value. The idea that transactional and transformational leadership are mutually exclusive (you can be one type or the other) may be too limiting. Better, perhaps, to say that sometimes one is appropriate, other times it is the other. This puts it more in line with the Bennis and Nanus approach, that both are needed – doing it right is not an alternative to doing the right thing, but a necessary part of it. Equally, a transformational relationship based on shared values and goals may need to be underpinned by a core transactional relationship to ensure that the basics of the job get done.

Reflection

What does leadership mean to you? Think about someone you know who you regard as an effective leader. What is it that that person does that you regard as demonstrating leadership? Which of these ideas about leadership does this relate to?

Did you come up with any other aspects that give you a clear idea of what leadership is, as well as the ability to:

- inspire others to follow in a particular direction
- make decisions in situations where there is uncertainty
- bring about movement or change in the desired direction?

It is quite possible that you identified some of the qualities that leaders need – the ability to communicate their vision, to understand other people – qualities that leaders possess. It is these qualities that we will move on to look at next, but they are the qualities that leaders need, rather than defining what leadership is. For the purposes of *Introducing Leadership*, we will treat leadership as being *the ability to bring about movement or change in a group or organization, when there is risk or uncertainty, by inspiring others to head in a particular direction*. Throughout the book we will return to this definition to explore how it shapes the role and behaviour of leaders and, in particular, the role and behaviour of leaders of teams, groups or sections within organizations.

15

Action centred leaders

Before we leave the question of 'What is leadership?' behind, there are a few other approaches to leadership that are worth considering, not because they contradict the definition we have just arrived at, but because they can help us to test out how well it works in practice. One of the UK's leading writers and teachers about leadership is John Adair. He usually appears in most of the lists of 'leadership gurus' and he has been influential in putting the study of leadership in the spotlight.

Adair's idea of action centred leadership arose out of his work with the Army, where he was involved in the development of officers as leaders, and in his later work in industry. Adair's approach is a much more practical one than discussions about 'doing the right thing' or 'doing it right', because he was concerned with the problems facing real leaders in the field or the factory. He argued that there are three dimensions to the leadership role, each of which needs to be taken account of in determining whether or not a leader is effective in the role. These dimensions are:

- the task
- the individual
- the team.

One of the first things to note about these three elements of the leadership role is how well they develop Lawrence Appley's definition of management that was introduced earlier ('getting things done through people'). The task is another way of saying 'getting things done' and the team and the individual are the people through whom these things are done. What Adair argues very strongly, and this was probably one of his lasting contributions to leadership, is that leadership involves a set of skills that can be learned. Leadership is not something you are either born with or without, but that most people can acquire leadership skills.

Key idea

Judging ideas

Effective leaders and managers have a range of valuable skills, as we will discover throughout this book. One is the ability to test out ideas and decide how useful they are to help resolve problems. There are very few hard and fast rules to guide you in making decisions, and some of the ideas that theorists and leadership 'gurus' present are contradictory. To be effective in your role you need to develop some practical tools to judge which ideas can help you, and one way of judging the effectiveness of any of them is to ask: 'How well does this fit with other ideas about this same topic?' The fact that John Adair's and Lawrence Appley's ideas do relate quite well is an indicator that they might both be on the right track.

Servant-leaders

Robert Greenleaf worked for most of his life at AT&T. After retirement, he began a second career teaching and consulting at institutions ranging from Harvard Business School to the Ford Foundation, as well as churches and other voluntary organizations. In some ways, his ideas echo Burns' ideas about the moral dimension of leadership, because Greenleaf believed that leaders could operate anywhere along a continuum ranging from those who put themselves first and are driven by their own need for power and to achieve personal goals, and those who are driven by the needs of others, to enable them to succeed and achieve, the 'servant-leaders'.

What Greenleaf saw was that many people may bring about change and development in organizations, communities and other settings and that they may do so without having formal leadership positions or, in fact, without wanting to be seen as having played a significant role. The key to servant-leadership is understanding others and working with them to achieve goals; using our definition of leadership, Greenleaf's servant-leaders *bring about movement or change in a group or organization* through harnessing the motivations and goals of those they lead, rather than attempting to sell them another vision, working with the grain of the people they lead rather than cutting across it.

Emotionally-intelligent leaders

In 1990, two American academics, John Mayer and Peter Salovey, published articles that brought the phrase 'emotional intelligence' into the public domain. It was picked up by a journalist called Daniel Goleman and led to his book, *Emotional Intelligence*, becoming a best-seller in 1995. Emotional intelligence is best thought of (according to Mayer and Salovey) as 'the ability to monitor one's own and others' emotions, to discriminate among them, and to use the information to guide one's thinking and actions'.

You can see that leadership, if it is all about *inspiring others to head in a particular direction*, demands that you have some insight into what will cause people to head in the desired direction. What is more, since people are driven as much by their emotions as they are by their rational analysis of the world about them, effective leadership must surely involve some degree of emotional awareness. If so, then we need to have some insight into what that involves.

We will look at emotional intelligence in more detail in Chapter 3, where we explore the skills that leaders need to perform effectively in the role. However, emotional intelligence has become very popular and may well be seen as the latest management gimmick. In fact, the basic ideas underpinning emotional intelligence (if not the name) have been around for decades, as part of the study of social psychology. What is more, the idea that leadership involves the emotions is one that has been around for even longer. When Queen Elizabeth I stood before her troops at Tilbury and said: 'I know I have the body but of a weak and feeble woman; but I have the heart and stomach of a king, and of a king of England too', she was inspiring her troops through a direct pull on their emotions. It is this aspect of leadership, the ability to bypass people's rational responses to what is being asked of them and appeal directly to their emotions, that is often described as 'charisma'. Charismatic figures, like Good Queen Bess or, in modern times, Che Guevara, John F. Kennedy and Nelson Mandela, have all excited their followers as much by who they were, as personalities, as they have by their deeds.

There are some similarities between the ideas of charismatic, emotionally intelligent and transformational leadership. The difficulty with charisma is that it is difficult to define or measure, but is generally recognized as the ability some people have to draw people to their particular vision and inspire them to follow by virtue of their personality. In particular, followers of charismatic leaders seem to believe that the leader is speaking directly to them, which fits in with the idea of emotional intelligence (the awareness of others' emotions and using this awareness to guide one's own behaviour). The transformational leader is also someone who operates very much at this emotional level, relying on confidence and trust to inspire followership rather than using more concrete appeals about the benefits that will accrue to the follower through 'transactions'.

Again, we will follow up on some of these ideas in Chapter 3, because the idea that charisma is central to leadership tends to imply that it is something that people are born with. In fact, as you will see, there are many skills and behaviours that people can acquire that enable you to develop your emotional intelligence. Although some people may find it hard to develop these skills fully, most of us can learn them and apply them to become effective leaders.

Leadership styles

So far we have developed an understanding of leadership that it is the ability to bring about movement or change in a group or organization, when there is risk or uncertainty, by inspiring others to head in a particular direction. We have contrasted this definition of leadership with the idea of management as being about planning, organizing, commanding, coordinating and controlling, what Kotter calls 'coping with complexity'. We have also suggested that an important aspect of leadership is the ability to connect with followers at an emotional level, and that it is this ability that is particularly noticeable in leaders who are described as charismatic. Finally, we have introduced the idea that leaders are people who are driven by some sense of what is morally right, an aspect of leadership that we will explore in more detail in the next chapter.

However, let us finish this chapter by considering one other aspect of leadership, leadership style, which is the ability to match how you lead people according to the circumstances you find yourself in. The most widely used way of describing how your style of leadership should adapt to the situation was developed by Paul Hersey and Kenneth Blanchard in their 1969 book *Management of Organizational Behaviour: Utilizing Human Resources* and is called (not surprisingly) Situational Leadership®[1].

They argue that the style of leadership you adopt should reflect the needs of the individual being led – the follower. To judge what is the most appropriate style you should assess the followers' levels of competence and commitment.

Competence, in this setting, means 'How able is the follower to perform the desired tasks?'; commitment is the follower's motivation or willingness to do it. You can see that there are four possible states that followers could be in (the labels D1 to D4 are Hersey and Blanchard's):

D1 Low in competence and commitment (cannot do the job and they do not feel that they should do it)

D2 Some competence but uncommitted (could do the job, but not well and are not really keen to)

D3 Fairly competent but not fully committed (could probably do a fair job, but lack the desire to)

D4 Highly competent and committed (is quite capable of getting on with the job on their own).

According to Hersey and Blanchard, the leader should respond to these four states by focusing on one or other of two behaviours:

- Supportive behaviour (to help develop competence)
- Directive behaviour (to counteract the lack of commitment).

For each of the four follower states, there are corresponding leadership styles (see Figure 1.3).

The difference between this approach to leadership and those we have looked at before is that it focuses very much on the skills leaders need and argues that how one leads should be dependent on who is being led. It is a useful guide to dealing with specific issues in relation to individuals – how much direction and support does this team member need to complete this task – but does not easily guide you as to how to deal with the whole team when their levels of competence and commitment may vary!

Follower's development level	Leadership style	
D1 Low in competence and commitment	S1 Directing	The leader tells the follower what to do and supervises work closely
D2 Some competence but uncommitted	S2 Coaching	Although still directing followers, they are allowed to participate more, but decisions still made by the leader
D3 Fairly competent but not fully committed	S3 Supporting	The leader allows the follower more freedom to decide what to do and how to do it, but supervises without being too controlling
D4 Highly competent and committed	S1 Delegating	By and large followers are left to make decisions on their own; they decide what help they want from the leader

Figure 1.3 Hersey and Blanchard's 'followership and leadership'

There is a similar model to Hersey and Blanchard's that was originally developed in 1961 by Robert Blake and Jane Mouton and published in their book *The Managerial Grid*, which may also remind you of John Adair's action centred leadership. The managerial grid suggests that the two key dimensions that shape leaders' behaviour are their focus on people and their focus on production (or the task). Some leaders (or managers – originally the model talked only about managers, but it is often spoken of as if it were about leadership) will focus more on one dimension, some on the other. Blake and Mouton argued that to be truly effective, it is important to be focused on both – ensuring that peoples' needs are met so that they are well motivated (or committed) and also that there is a clear focus on the task that needs doing and how it has to be done (their competence).

Rather than looking at these (and other) theories as being in conflict, it soon becomes clear that they are often concentrating on different aspects of the same thing. Both models emphasize that there is no 'one size fits all' way of leading people, and that you need to be sensitive to the needs of the people you lead, and adjust your behaviour accordingly. Whereas Hersey and Blanchard make the point that it is people's commitment and competence that you should be concerned about, Blake and Mouton are saying that the leader should be looking at both the people and the task that needs completing. What is to stop you considering commitment and competence when you look at people, especially as the level of competence must be closely linked to the task?

What this suggests is that leadership is not a simple, two-dimensional issue, it is far more complex than that. What different models can help you do is structure your thinking to make your task a little easier by focusing attention on different aspects.

Balancing leadership and management

The argument of *Introducing Leadership* is quite straightforward – leadership and management are not alternatives, one is not 'better' than the other, nor are they the same thing. Instead, the argument is that leadership and management are different aspects of the same basic role, but that they focus on different aspects of the role. All managers need to be effective leaders, and all leaders need to be effective managers. However, the relative importance

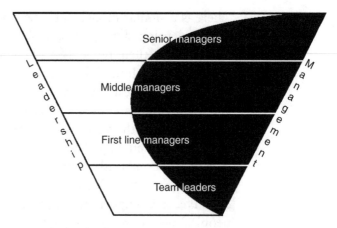

Figure 1.4   The leadership/management role relationship

of the two aspects will vary according to the specific circumstances and also because of the role that a person occupies.

In particular, the leadership and the management demands of a role will differ between different levels in the same organization. Figure 1.4 illustrates how this variation is likely to occur.

The idea behind this diagram is that the balance of leadership and management alters according to the nature of the role, but that people at all levels in organizations will need both sets of skills – to manage and to lead.

The chief executive of any organization, above all else, has to provide the leadership – the sense of direction – that the organization needs, and to ensure that it is responsive to the external environment in which it operates – to enable it to move forward and change. At this level there is maximum uncertainty and risk:

- what will happen to the economy?
- how will our customers behave?
- what will our competitors do?
- what legal or political developments might affect us?

This is where leadership is absolutely critical and where it is hardest to plan, to control, etc., because the external environment is subject to far too many forces.

Conversely, team leaders who are part of the team being led, who do the same work as the other members of their teams and have very little real managerial responsibility appear to work in a very stable environment. Yet, they also have to put the focus on leadership, but at a very specific level of operation. They have to ensure that the team is working to clear goals, that they are heading in the direction they should be heading and that they respond to the detailed changes that affect them daily or even hourly, as priorities are changed by others, over whom they have no control – their suppliers, their customers and their line managers.

These team leaders have no real authority or power other than through their own personal ability to lead, do not engage in much planning above the day to day, control very little, and command even less. They do have to coordinate what is being done and they may organize what members of the team do, and when, but they are not really managers, they are leaders of their teams.

It is at the intermediate stages, from first line managers up to more senior 'middle managers' that the main task of management occurs, but it is also here that leadership is required. *Introducing Leadership* is written explicitly for people working at this level, especially those who are described as 'First Line Managers'. They may be called team leaders, they may be called supervisors or line managers, but they are the people who have to ensure that the organization's operations run smoothly. (The Appendix has more detailed descriptions of the different levels of management; use them to help you identify where you fit into these levels.)

The distinctions between the different levels of management in the diagram are not carved in stone, nor are the names clear-cut. Some organizations call quite senior managers 'Team Leaders' – here the term is reserved for leaders of operational teams in the factory, office or warehouse. Many first line managers are also called team leaders, although they are also regarded as being part of the organization's management structure. As Humpty Dumpty said in *Through the Looking Glass*: 'When *I* use a word, it means just what I choose it to mean – neither more nor less'. In *Introducing Leadership* we use the terms 'first line manager' and 'middle manager' to mean those members of the organization's management who have responsibility for, and are accountable for, putting the organization's strategy into operation.

They will have a very distinct management role and, what is most important, they will also have to blend this with effective leadership. As the population has become better educated, as people have learned to ask questions and challenge received wisdom, the

23

workforces of most organizations are less willing to accept what is often called 'command and control' management. They want to know 'Why?' They want to have a chance to take responsibility for their own actions and to have a say in what is done and how it is done. All this means that people want leadership as well as (not instead of) management. They want to have their hearts and their minds engaged, and that requires real, effective leadership. That is what *Introducing Leadership* is all about, but it is also why it sits side by side with *Introducing Management*, because the two roles sit side by side as well.

Summary

- Management has been defined as being about planning, organizing, commanding, coordinating and controlling, using Henri Fayol's classic definition.

- Leadership has been defined as 'the ability to bring about movement or change in a group or organization, when there is risk or uncertainty, by inspiring others to head in a particular direction'.

- The balance between 'leading' and 'managing' may vary at different levels in an organization, but all managers need to lead to be effective (and effective leaders need to be able to manage).

- Different approaches to leadership have been explored and their similarities highlighted, especially their focus on leaders being able to relate well to, communicate with and inspire people in order to get results, and that this requires various skills that can be learnt and applied as the circumstances demand.

Note

1 The name Situational Leadership® is a trademark of the Centre for Leadership Studies, which is headed by Paul Hersey. Both he and Ken Blanchard (who also wrote *The One Minute Manager*) run and license training courses based on the model.

2   Leadership and ethics

In Chapter 1 you saw that James MacGregor Burns said that 'divorced from ethics, leadership is reduced to management'. Although the idea that management is an ethics-free zone is not one that any competent manager would support, nevertheless, it emphasizes that ethical considerations play a significant part in effective leadership. This chapter will explore why that is and just what it means in developing yourself as a leader.

What are 'ethics'?

The study of ethics is a branch of philosophy that attempts to understand the nature of morality (which is why it is sometimes called moral philosophy) – in other words, it tries to distinguish what is right from what is wrong. Ethics is a very large and challenging area to explore, so we will confine ourselves to some core ethical issues that all leaders need to consider. These are:

- what do we mean by right (as in 'do the right thing')?
- what do I do when my idea about what is right conflicts with yours?

You may well ask why this is only relevant to leaders – shouldn't we all try to do the right thing, and don't we all get faced with conflicts between what we believe is right and what others believe? Yes, of course we do, but leaders are different. Their role requires that they make decisions about what to do that others follow – they set the direction in which people go and the standard by which their performance is judged. When a leader says 'This is right', it means that other people are living with that judgement. That is why leaders must be very clear about their personal standards of morality, so that:

- they know where to draw the line (to give them certainty in making decisions)

25

- to avoid inconsistency (so that others will have confidence in them)
- to reduce their own doubts and confidence.

Reflection

How confident are you in your own sense of morality – what is right and wrong? Where or how did you develop this ability to judge yourself and others' behaviour? Has your assessment of what is right or wrong changed over time? If so, how and why?

People develop their personal sense of morality – of what is right or wrong – from many sources, but the earliest influences are most definitely their family, the social environment in which they grow up (their local community, their religion, etc.) and the wider culture of which they are a part. This process is called 'socialization'. We learn how to be part of society by learning the rules that govern society, and some of those rules are about what is right or wrong.

You may believe that the rules about morality are given to us by God (e.g. the ten commandments) and, because of that, are unchanging. You may believe that these rules come from a fundamental set of individual rights that establishes what is right (you must not kill or steal because people have a right to life and to own property), or you may believe that these rules exist to enable us to coexist (I won't harm you if you don't harm me). This chapter is not about which of these sources of morality you should subscribe to. Instead it emphasizes that, to be an effective leader, you must be clear what your basic sense of right and wrong is and feel confident to make judgements based on those rules. Of course, not everyone shares your ideas about right and wrong; different societies have different rules, as Figure 2.1 illustrates.

What Trompenaars shows, in this example, is how different perceptions of what is right or wrong are firmly based in the culture in which people grow up. The dominant culture of northern Europe and North America is one in which the rule of law over-rides the obligations to family, friends and the social group of which you are part. For the Korean manager he quotes, this is quite wrong. Obligations to one's social group over-ride obligations to wider

A leading authority on the effects of cultural diversity in globalized business, Fons Trompenaars, uses a simple exercise to illustrate how differences in what we believe is right or wrong can hamper effective business relationships. In his book *Did the pedestrian die?* he explains the problem. You are with a close friend. He is driving above the speed limit and hits a pedestrian; could your friend expect you to protect him?

Trompenaars offers three possibilities:

- Yes, he has a definite right
- He has some right
- He has no right

Most northern Europeans and North Americans would say no, especially once they learn that the pedestrian died. Southern Europeans, South Americans and Asians are more likely to say yes, he could expect to be protected. For the first group, this is evidence of immorality on the part of the second group. Equally, the second group sees the first as being immoral. As one Korean is quoted as having said to Trompenaars: 'I knew Americans were corrupt but you gave it empirical evidence, thank you.' When asked how, he replied: 'You can't trust Americans, they don't even help their friends.'

Figure 2.1   Different societies have different rules about right and wrong

society, to strangers. This is how our perceptions of right and wrong can lead us to reach very different decisions while appealing to the same basic principle – we should do this because it is right!

This is why ethics is so important to leaders, whatever their specific role. In the diverse society that we live in, the old certainties that everyone would share the same basic beliefs in what is right and what is wrong are not there any more. Different religions, an absence of religious beliefs, a range of different moral standards, make it hard to be certain how different people will judge specific problems.

To be effective, leaders need to be clear about the moral basis on which their decisions are made. They also have to be able to recognize differences in others' moral decisions and understand why they differ and how to respond to them. In this chapter we will explore these issues and look at some real-life events that have tested leaders' ability to make judgements about what is right and what is wrong.

Right and wrong

As you learned in Chapter 1, one of the very common ways of distinguishing between leadership and management is between 'doing the right thing' and 'doing things right' (that is between transformational and transactional leadership). We also empha-sized that the word 'right' tends to be used in two different ways:

- right as being correct
- right as being ethical.

Although these two meanings can overlap, there is an important difference. Right as correct implies that there is some sort of objec-tive measure as to whether something is correct or not. For example, the statement that:

It is illegal to decide not to promote a woman to team leader simply because some of the men in the team would not want to be led by a woman.

is right (correct) – it is illegal to discriminate against women in this way. There is a set of criteria that we can use to judge a statement like this, and these criteria are spelled out in the words of the Equal Opportunities Act and in decisions about the implementa-tion of the law made by Employment Tribunals. 'Doing things right' is all about making sure that decisions on promoting people are made in ways that put the best person into the job, and do not break the law. You do not have to believe in the law for the decision you make to be correct under the law – to do things right.

But suppose that you believe that it would endanger the whole future of your organization if someone were to be promoted, as it would cause some male employees to leave, men who would be nearly impossible to replace because of severe skills shortages. Should you do the legally correct thing or should you take other fac-tors into account? Do you believe that it is better to break the law because it is 'doing the right thing'? Is it right to promote a particu-lar woman to a role, because she is probably the best for the post, when several perfectly suitable (male) alternatives have also applied, when you know that key personnel would leave and that this, in turn, would make it almost impossible to deliver a contract that may well cause the company to collapse, putting everyone out of work?

Before you read further, think about this situation and see which of the statements in Figure 2.2 you most agree with.

You may have thought that the answer is obvious, or you may have felt torn between two different statements, and found it dif-ficult to choose. Which is the correct answer? There isn't one. Any question that asks, 'What ought I to do?' can only be answered in

> 1 Even if this were not illegal, I would never make a judgement like this, because it is wrong to discriminate on the grounds of someone's sex.
>
> 2 Although I can accept that there is a good case to be made for discriminating, I would not do so because it is illegal.
>
> 3 I would have great difficulty in discriminating in this way, especially as it is illegal, although I can see that it may be the right thing to do in the circumstances.
>
> 4 I think it probably makes sense to appoint someone who would be more likely to assure the future of all employees, despite it being at the expense of one individual and being illegal because, on balance, it is for the greater good of all.
>
> 5 It is perfectly sensible to ignore the law and appoint the person who is most likely to get on well with the rest of the team and who will make the future of the organization more certain, for the benefit of all employees.

Figure 2.2   What is your ethical position?

terms of what you believe is right. However, the example does allow us to explore two very different ways of applying your belief in what is right or wrong. The first answer (which lies at one extreme) is a good example of a way of approaching ethical issues that says, 'You should always do the right thing, whatever the consequences'. By contrast, the fifth option reflects a point of view that says the only true test of the rightness of an action is its effect. These two approaches have technical names, but they can just as easily be thought of in the following terms:

- always do what is right, come what may (technically, a *deontological* approach)

- the ends justify the means (technically, a *consequentialist* approach).

The first of these approaches would justify any action on the grounds that this is the right thing to do, according to the moral rules that guide our behaviour. It is easiest to appreciate it by looking at the kind of situations that a manager might be faced with:

1 A team member is found to be buying products at a discount for someone else, which is against the rules, as employees can only get staff discount on items for their own use. The 'culprit' explains that his neighbour is very elderly and cannot afford to buy the item, so he was doing it to help her out.

2 A team member has swapped shifts without permission, to be able to visit her husband in hospital, and has clocked in using the other person's time card.

3 A box of components has been brought down to the line to be used despite there being a higher than acceptable level of rejects because the line would stop and orders couldn't be fulfilled if these components were not used.

So what would you do in each case? Would you report the person buying an item on behalf of poor neighbour (technically it is stealing)? Would you report the person swapping shifts (falsifying records)? Accept faulty components and supply goods when you know that too many are likely to be defective (possibly fraudulent behaviour)? All three behaviours involve ethical decisions and you may believe that a moral person should take action to prevent wrongdoing, despite the fact that it helps the poor, does no real harm to the business and ensures that orders get met with items that are mainly OK. If you cannot accept that you should do the wrong thing because it produces the right result, then that is what is meant by the deontological approach.

You would be in good company. This approach was argued by the German philosopher Immanuel Kant and the English philosopher John Locke, although not for precisely the same reasons. There are some powerful consequences of this sort of approach. Many religious and political martyrs have suffered for holding on to their beliefs, despite the consequences. They believed that knowing what was right prevented them from taking the easy way out of renouncing their views in order to live or be free. That is not to say that this approach always presents challenges, but it does mean that sometimes you must take a stand when everyone else says, 'But look at the consequences!'.

Standing up for what you believe is the right thing to do, come what may, demands strong personal confidence and usually causes people to respect you, but it can also make you unpopular. This is why you are more likely to be someone who believes that we should look at the effects of what we do when making judgements about what is right and are likely to work with people who share that belief. This consequentialist approach (because it considers the consequence) tends to focus on the greater good; in the discrimination case it might place the good of the organization above the good of the individual. By and large people tend to use this kind of judgement on a day-to-day basis; if I do that what effect would it have? If it produces the right effect then it must be the right thing to do.

Although this seems to be reasonable and pragmatic, it does present problems:

- Not all effects are easy to predict, and there may be several, making it necessary to balance the good against the bad.

- Presented with a similar problem in the future, you may make a different decision because the effects proved to be wrong, making you appear inconsistent.

- To those who cannot see the effect, you may appear to be behaving in ways that they regard as immoral.

If all this appears to be arguing that the consequentialist approach is wrong, it isn't. What is being argued is that there are challenges with both approaches; always doing what you think is right, come what may, can produce unwelcome results; always considering the effects of actions and making decisions accordingly may not always work and may make you appear inconsistent.

Is there an alternative? In reality, quite a few people use both approaches – they will have certain fundamental beliefs that they try to abide by in all their decisions, while judging each problem on its own terms. This attempt to balance 'always doing what is right' with a pragmatic approach, when the effects of doing so seem to be more harmful than seems reasonable, is the way most people deal with the world (Figure 2.3).

Doing the right thing

How can you, as a leader, make sure you always do the right thing? Start by being clear what your basic beliefs and values are, your views of what is right or wrong. Some values, like not killing or harming others (except in self-defence or the defence of others) may be the most significant, but are rarely going to be needed to

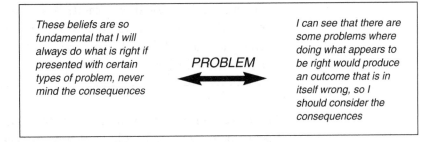

These beliefs are so fundamental that I will always do what is right if presented with certain types of problem, never mind the consequences

PROBLEM

I can see that there are some problems where doing what appears to be right would produce an outcome that is in itself wrong, so I should consider the consequences

Figure 2.3   Making ethical decisions

guide our behaviour at work. There are some others that are far more significant in your day-to-day work, such as:

- Honesty, in both your words (what you say to people) and deeds (not taking what is not yours)
- Equity (without favouritism of prejudice) and fairness (as their own behaviour demands) in the way that you treat people
- Integrity (doing what you believe is right) and consistency (applying the same rule in the same way) to demonstrate your beliefs through your behaviour.

To help you reflect on your own values and sense of what is right or wrong, as a leader, look at the following questions and think about what you believe to be the right thing to do.

Reflection

Honesty   Are there any circumstances where you would not tell the truth, as far as you know it? If there are, what are they and why would you not tell the truth? In particular, would you simply say nothing or would you tell a lie? Why? Are there any circumstances where you would take what is not yours (either personally or your team's or department's)? If there are, what are they, and why would you do this?

Equity   Are there any reasons why you might treat one person differently from another? Do you believe that it is fair to discriminate between people on the basis of features over which they have some control (their behaviour, or their beliefs) but not over features that they cannot change (their race, sex, physical disability)?

Integrity   Do you ever have to make decisions or behave in ways at work that you do not feel happy about, because you believe they are not always right? What are these; why do you do this? Do you always make decisions and behave consistently at work? What do you think other people would say about these variations?

There are no right or wrong answers to these questions. If it were easy to be honest, equitable and show integrity in all we do, then there would be little to say about them. Doing the right thing is never easy, but to be effective as a leader you need to be aware of what the right thing is and make every effort to live to the standard you expect from others. This is what philosophers call the *golden rule*, because it is found in nearly every belief system in nearly every culture – treat other people the way that you want them to treat you. As a leader, it is your responsibility to set the example for others to follow.

When leaders go wrong

In order to understand how people can make decisions that, subsequently, prove to have been disastrous, let us look at some examples of organizations brought down by poor leadership. These leaders were chief executives, not first line or middle managers, but we will go on to examine the lessons that can be learnt from these cases.

The late nineties and the early part of the 21st century saw some spectacular business crashes in both the UK and USA – WorldCom, Global Crossing, Equitable Life and Marconi – but the most spectacular was Enron, which not only brought down the company but also the accountants Arthur Andersen, who were its auditors and advisors. What went wrong at Enron?

The Chairman and Chief Executive, Kenneth Lay, assisted by ideas man Jeffrey Shilling, who briefly succeeded his boss after the business went into financial meltdown, created what has been described as an 'asset-lite' company. The energy business (which Enron was in) was big business, usually involving large amounts of capital tied up in exploration, generation or storage. What Enron did was to expand not just its operations in the utilities industry (it bought Wessex Water in the UK, for example) but also acted as a market maker, buying and selling energy as an intermediary between producers and users. Such intermediaries use the price mechanism on both sides of the market, making a profit on the margins between what producers will sell at and customers will pay, a profit that is related in part to the risk they take in taking positions (setting prices and buying or selling volumes which they may or may not actually have at the time).

But Enron did not stop at gas or oil – it also set up markets in pollution rights, paper pulp and speciality chemicals. The company even got involved in swap and option contracts based on the weather, to provide a hedge against sharp changes that might affect agriculture or demands for power.

One problem with this twin track strategy was that expanding production capability demands high levels of investment which increase debt, whereas acting as a market maker means having high levels of credit to give trading partners confidence in Enron's ability to meet their commitments. It was this conflict that led to the creation of apparently independent entities, through which debt was hidden, in order to ensure that the balance sheet looked healthy, keeping the company's credit rating high.

Key idea

A company's balance sheet, along with its profit and loss account, is a primary record of the company's financial status. It shows what the company owns (its assets) and what it owes (its liabilities). Unfortunately, whether or not an asset or liability appears on a company's balance sheet is largely a matter of choice. For example, a company may choose to buy new equipment through bank borrowing. This creates a liability and adds to its assets. Alternatively, the asset could be leased for a fixed period, and so not appear on the balance sheet at all, as it remains the property of the finance company. Why does this matter? Because the scale of bank lending relative to the money invested by shareholders (equity capital) is regarded as a key measure of risk. This ratio, of equity to loan capital, is called *gearing* and indicates how risk is being shared between the owners and the company's creditors.

What Enron did was more sophisticated than simply lease assets. It was engaged in complicated financial transactions, buying and selling energy (gas, oil, electricity) to balance supply and demand between producers and consumers or, to be more precise, suppliers to domestic and commercial users. This is a high-risk enterprise, as 'promises' of future supplies are bought and sold, with the intermediary taking a profit on the difference between the prices as a reward for shouldering the risk.

Much of this trading is done by initially paying only a small part of the value of the trade, so that the capital tied up in the options (to buy or sell at a fixed price) was only a fraction of the true liability or asset acquired. What is more, the profitability of the trades tends to be directly related to the risk, so the largest profits go to those who take the greatest risks – as do the greatest potential losses. What Enron did was to create separate companies through which the highest risk trades were placed. By injecting small amounts of capital, large risks could be taken which were not reflected in Enron's own accounts.

Enron was the darling of the markets, producing large dividends and share price increases for its investors (increasing what is called 'shareholder value'). It is this pressure, constantly striving to increase shareholder value, that can tend to lead to a dangerously short-term attitude in the way that organizations are run, in which growth and profits become an end in themselves, rather than a basis for creating a sustainable long-term business. If this is coupled to over-generous reward systems for Chief Executives, which are only loosely connected to performance (measured, of course, in terms of share prices and profits) and who only spend short periods in the job (in big public companies, most last less than four years), then there is little incentive to invest for the long term.

Reflection

If you had some money to invest in buying shares, what would you be using to judge a potential company by? Would it be the financial rewards it offers (shareholder value) or would you want to know about the ethics of the senior managers running the business? Given the choice, would you rather invest in an ethically run business that may not make much money, or one that was very profitable and appeared to be run lawfully (which is not necessarily the same as being run ethically)?

Many people have argued that the problem at Enron (and at the other companies that collapsed around the same time) was the kind of market capitalism that we see in the UK and USA (often called the Anglo-Saxon approach), in which the need to provide high levels of return to shareholders is the driver for business leaders. In many other European countries, the systems in place are designed to give at least as much weight to the needs of others (employees, the wider society), with much greater regulation and control by the state. Most finance is supplied by bank lending rather than shareholders, and those banks then have their own representatives sitting on supervisory boards alongside representatives of the employees, to monitor managers' behaviour.

Those people who believe strongly that the market is the best mechanism for controlling business are very much influenced by consequentialism – the end justifies the means. They argue that the market works best in deciding how organizations should operate, and that when things go wrong (as they did at Enron, Marconi, etc.), it is an exception to the general rule, and one that makes the market stronger (investors will be more careful in future). In the long run, the market produces better outcomes than any other mechanism (like regulation and state control) and so it is the *right* way to do things. On balance, and in total, it produces better results (market enthusiasts believe).

It is all about leadership

What caused Enron to go bust, and what led Arthur Andersen to fall with it, was poor leadership. This is easier to see if we compare Enron to a British organization, Equitable Life, because at Equitable Life many of the characteristics of Enron were absent. Equitable Life was a mutual organization, a bit like a cooperative, owned by the people who bought its life assurance policies, unit trusts and other savings and investment products. There were no investment bankers encouraging headlong spending sprees on takeovers, there was no need to ensure that shareholders got growth in their share prices and larger and larger dividends because there were no shareholders to satisfy. So what made Equitable Life go off the rails?

It seems that Equitable's CEOs, first Roy Ranson and then his protégé Alan Nash, who was also Equitable's Actuary (the professional responsible for assessing risk) had been bitten by the same bug of self-belief and reluctance to listen to doubters that affected Kenneth Lay and Jeffrey Shilling at Enron, Bernie Ebbers at WorldCom, Gary Winnick at Global Crossing, and George Simpson at Marconi (the other big name crashes). Ranson and Nash embarked on a major campaign of expansion to make Equitable a major player in the industry, not just by giving unrealistic guarantees to policy-holders but, as a recent report has discovered, by paying out bonuses to policy-holders that were not justified by the returns being earned. Such a strategy wrecked Marconi, WorldCom and Global Crossing, believing that growth is an end in itself and that the market will keep on growing because it has to, to justify the strategies being pursued.

This is not what leadership is about. Effective leadership is not about over-confidence and demanding blind loyalty, which seemed to be a common feature of these organizations' bosses. Leadership involves being open to questioning and challenge, from others and from yourself, without being plagued by them. Leadership means recognizing that the world is an uncertain place and that confidence comes from being aware of the risks and allowing for them, not ignoring them. A good leader takes a compass and map, but also takes a survival kit just in case – and makes sure that the rest of the party has one too.

This is where ethics come in, because leaders who are honest and have integrity will ask questions and look at the reality of what is happening in their organizations, not see only what they want to see. If they are fair and equitable in the way that they treat people, then people will feel safe to tell them the truth and not what they think leaders want to hear. That is not to say that leadership is about caution, quite the reverse. Good leaders take risks because they understand the risk and have allowed for it in their plans. Unfortunately, poor leaders – and that is what all these organizations suffered from – treat risks as something that only lesser mortals fear and keep going heedlessly, but then cause those same lesser mortals (their employees and shareholders) to pay the price of their lack of caution.

People trust leaders who take risks if they show, by word and deed, that the risks have been assessed and that the path being followed is the right one. Most importantly of all, that those leaders are sharing the risks that others are being asked to take and are not cocooned in share options, pension rights and employment contracts that ensure that no matter what happens, they will not suffer in the same way that those they lead may have to suffer. Trust comes not from always being right, but by showing that your self-belief is tempered by an appreciation of the implications of your actions on others, and not asking anyone to do something that you would not do yourself.

The lessons for all leaders

You do not have to be a chief executive to learn from Enron or Equitable Life. Managers and leaders at all levels in organizations can behave in exactly the same way, sometimes with equally disastrous consequences. Nick Leeson was a trader and manager at a small office of Barings Bank, based in Singapore. His actions managed to ruin Britain's oldest, and one of its most prestigious, merchant banks, and he did it in much the same way as Kenneth Lay or Roy Ranson. Leeson made a bad decision, and then tried to hide it by making more of the same kind of decisions. Because he was unsupervised (he was actually responsible for supervising his own work), there was nobody to challenge what he had done.

Instead of recognizing that he was making a bad situation worse, Leeson went on digging the hole he was in, first deceiving himself and then deceiving others. That is the lesson that all leaders need to learn. If you have a personal set of values that you are conscious of and which shape your behaviour, including values such as honesty, integrity, equity and fairness, then you will find that it is much easier to deal with the problems you meet at work in ways that produce the right sorts of results. For example:

- Honesty means that you will tell people what you are doing and discuss the consequences.

- Integrity means that you will ask people for their views and listen to what they say, but make your own decisions and stand by them.

- Equity and fairness means that you will treat people with respect, listen to what they say, even if you do not want to hear it, and act in ways that demonstrate this.

This does not mean you will always be right. It does mean that you will recognize when you are wrong and learn from it. The lesson from Enron, Equitable Life and the others is that their leaders there did not want to face the truth of the situation until it was forced on them. By then it was too late to do anything about it.

Social responsibility

Do employers have a responsibility to society as well as to their shareholders? Should they be concerned about the conditions that their employees work in? Should they be concerned about the conditions that their suppliers' employees work in? Should they be concerned about the environmental impact of their activities? Should they be concerned about the effect of their activities on the world's future climate?

Some of these questions are dealt with by the law (Health and Safety at Work Act, Environmental Protection Act, etc.), but all are ethical questions, since they start with the word 'should', and 'should' means that this is a question involving moral judgements. So, what should you do if you believe that your employer is breaking the law, or doing something that is legal but is wrong? For example:

- Your employer has a set of safe working practices that are very difficult to observe, so most managers turn a blind eye, because the actual risk is very low, even if the consequences could be severe (in term of severe injury or death).

- The factory generates a lot of waste and it is difficult to get rid of some of it. A contractor is prepared to take it, no questions asked, and you believe it is being disposed of illegally.

- Your employer imports goods from South-East Asia. They are produced in factories staffed by prisoners, who are paid nothing, making the cost very low.

- Employees of a local council make home visits and are paid a car allowance to do so, despite there being good public transport available, which leads to higher levels of carbon emissions, affecting the world's climate.

What should you do? It is hard to be the odd one out in an organization that accepts that it is right to behave in a way that you do not believe is right. As a leader and manager, do you have a responsibility to do something to change how your employer operates? There are four possible strategies you can pursue:

Silent campaigner	The best thing to do is to try to fit in as best you can, and hope to change it from inside, without making a fuss.
Moral benchmark	Without trying to be confrontational, make it clear that you will not do anything that you believe is wrong, and set an example that you hope others will follow, within your own area of responsibility.
Grit in the oyster	Stand up for what you believe is right, challenging other managers to change their ways and demonstrating clearly the behaviour you think they should also exhibit.
Whistleblower	Report the breaches to the appropriate authorities or to campaigning groups, supplying them with the information they need to prosecute the employer or publicize the behaviour.

Which is the right way to behave? Only you can decide, depending on your own convictions about what is right, the consequences of your actions, and the likelihood of them having any effect. You have certain legal obligations to report unlawful behaviour (breaching health and safety or environmental discharge laws, for example) and you are protected in whistleblowing by the 1999 Public Interest Disclosure Act. The advice and information service, Public Concern at Work, who help people who believe that there is a need to blow the whistle on some aspect of an organization's behaviour, offer the advice in Figure 2.4 to potential whistleblowers[1].

Should a leader behave in an underhand way, by reporting an organization anonymously? Shouldn't a leader stand up publicly and tell the world what is going on? In theory, it sounds fine to risk your livelihood to expose wrongdoing, and there are certainly good reasons for doing so, but equally, people with dependants, who would like to have a career in the future, may well feel that discretion is the better part of valour. So long as the problem is reported to those able to do something, then they have done what is needed. Being an effective leader, behaving in an ethically sound way, does not mean having to be a romantic hero. There are many different ways to 'do the right thing' and your role is to choose what seems to you to be the most appropriate one. Doing nothing when you see that things are wrong is never the right thing, that's for certain!

Actions not words

Some organizations make a public effort to abide by high ethical standards, what is often called corporate social responsibility. One well-known example is The Body Shop. It has a very public position

Do	Don't
• Keep calm	• Forget there may be an innocent or good explanation
• Think about the risks and outcomes before you act	• Become a private detective
• Remember you are a witness, not a complainant	• Use a whistleblowing procedure to pursue a personal grievance
• Phone Public Concern at Work for advice	• Expect thanks

Figure 2.4   'Dos' and 'Don'ts' of whistle-blowing

on some significant social issues, expressed through its statement of corporate values (Figure 2.5)[2].

There is nothing new in this; organizations have been driven by a set of underpinning ethical standards for many years.

- In 1800, mill manager Robert Owen transformed life in the village of New Lanark by abolishing child labour and corporal punishment and providing his employees with decent homes, schools and evening classes, free health care, and affordable food.

- In 1861, George and Richard Cadbury, members of a Quaker family, took over their family cocoa business. Eighteen years later they built a new factory and a village to house their workers at Bourneville. They built a school, hospital, reading rooms and wash-houses and the company also introduced Saturday half days and Bank Holiday closing, and provided a wide variety of sporting and recreational facilities for their employees.

- Another Quaker and successful businessman, Joseph Rowntree, took over his father's grocery shop in 1859 and, 10 years later, joined his brother in founding the business that became Rowntree. In 1904 he built the garden village of New Earswick to provide decent homes for factory workers to live in.

What these examples show is that adopting an ethical approach to business does not mean that an organization is disadvantaged, quite the reverse. By ensuring that they employed healthy, well-educated people, Owen, Cadbury and Rowntree gained commercial advantage as well as doing what they believed was morally right.

- We consider testing products or ingredients on animals to be morally and scientifically indefensible.
- We support small producer communities around the world who supply us with accessories and natural ingredients.
- We know that you're unique, and we'll always treat you like an individual. We like you just the way you are.
- We believe that it is the responsibility of every individual to actively support those who have human rights denied to them.
- We believe that a business has the responsibility to protect the environment in which it operates, locally and globally.

Figure 2.5 The Body Shop's values

41

The idea that organizations should be driven by ethical values is not something that is exclusive to the private sector. Most public sector organizations – local councils, hospitals, schools, etc. – would argue that their value systems are critical to their effectiveness in meeting the needs of their local communities, their patients and their pupils. Equally, organizations in the voluntary and mutual sector (sometimes called the third sector) are particularly driven by values. Organizations like charities, cooperatives, trades unions and building societies, all have particular sets of values that underpin their operations.

As a manager and leader in any type of organization you need to be aware of its values. These may be expressed in a values statement (as The Body Shop does), or it may be that you have to reflect on the way that the organization operates and how senior managers make their decisions (the organization's culture or 'how we do things around here'). Two key questions you need to ask are:

- How well do any public statements of the organization's values coincide with the way it actually operates (do senior managers 'walk the walk as well as talk the talk')?

- How well do the organization's values coincide with your own (do you believe in what it is trying to do and to be)?

Where conflicts occur between either of these positions, you will find that you are faced with ethical dilemmas in your working life. When faced with such dilemmas the strength of your ethical commitments becomes critical. Only you can decide what you believe is right, and how far you will go in doing the right thing. However, other people will judge you on the basis of how well you match your words and your actions, and your success as a leader will depend on these judgements. You need to reflect on this; the consequence of such conflicts is something we will return to in Chapter 9.

Summary

- Being ethical is about doing what you believe is right – effective leaders do not try to please everyone by developing a morality that will not offend (that is impossible). Instead, they are very clear about their own moral standards, they make an effort to discuss these with others and listen to their viewpoint, and then make decisions that they believe in. That is the basis for ethics in leadership.

- Doing the right thing involves making decisions about how you define 'what is right'. Is it about certain beliefs or values that should shape your behaviour, come what may, or does the end justify the means, should you assess the effect of your behaviour in judging what is right?

- The key aspects of ethics in leadership are honesty, integrity, equity and fairness. The worst leaders are those who hide from the truth of their actions and only listen to those who tell them what they want to hear. Effective leaders welcome the truth, however unpleasant it is, and admit when they are going the wrong way.

- Organizations that try to live by ethical standards, by adopting socially responsible policies and publicizing their values, can be just as economically successful as those that do not. You should judge an organization's values by how it behaves, make your own ethical judgements as to how well it lives up to its own standards and to yours, and act according to your beliefs.

Notes

1 To get help from Public Concern at Work visit their website, http://www.pcaw.co.uk or call their helpline 020 7404 6609.
2 You can find out more about these values and what The Body Shop does to translate them into action by visiting their website, (http://www.uk.thebodyshop.com) and clicking on 'our values'.

3 Leadership and character

In Chapter 1 we looked at what is meant by leadership and Chapter 2 explored the role of ethics in leadership. This Chapter looks at the role of character or, at least, the personal characteristics that effective leaders possess. It starts with the simple principle that most people can learn to be leaders and rejects the common belief that leaders are 'born and not made'. It was once thought that leaders were a special breed and that only a few were born to lead. This 'great man' theory (and it was assumed that leaders could only be men) had the big advantage of only allowing a certain 'class' of men to become leaders. If the ability to lead was somehow innate, it was likely to be inherited, so only the sons of leaders could become leaders. That was why the army did not need to train its officers and allowed them to buy their commissions – they would have the ability to lead because they could afford to become officers!

What is 'character'?

This idea of leadership is similar to what is now called 'trait theory'. A trait is a characteristic that a person has which tends to be associated with a particular type of behaviour. The assumption of the trait theory of leadership is that people have a set of traits – characteristics – that enable them to be effective leaders. What do we mean by characteristics? This can be used to mean different things. Some people would include physical characteristics as traits (people's physical size or racial characteristics), but in the trait theory of leadership, the traits they were talking about were essentially personality traits – different aspects of someone's personality.

It was once thought (and still is, by some people), that a certain 'class' of people would naturally possess these traits. Today, many people still feel that leadership is something that people have or have not got, and that the most that anyone can do is to polish up that ability to make the best of it. *Introducing Leadership* has argued that leadership is the ability to inspire followership, to bring about change, make decisions and to provide direction. So are these abilities that only some people have, or are they abilities that most of us can develop, at least to a degree? The argument is that 'Yes, they can be developed' and in this chapter we will look at the 'characteristics' that make an effective leader – the personality traits, abilities and other personal qualities they are likely to need. Chapter 4 then goes on to look at the personal skills that leaders must have to enable them to draw on their personal characteristics most effectively.

Is 'character' just about personality? No, personality is only one aspect. Character covers several different but interrelated aspects of people that shape their behaviour and their relationships with others. It includes:

- personality
- attitudes
- personal motivation
- emotional intelligence.

You have probably come across some or all of these terms before, and may have your own ideas about what they mean. You may also think that they are much the same or that they are related to each other in some way, in which you would be partially right. They do have important differences but they do interrelate, in that some will have a significant impact on the others. Our starting place will be personality traits, partly because they are largely fixed and because it used to be thought that they defined leadership.

Personality traits

What is meant by personality? It is easier to understand the word if we think about how it is used in general conversation. We may describe someone as having a 'pleasant (or awkward) personality', or of 'being personable' – in other words, personality is the word we use to describe how someone relates to other people, as a person. Are they forthcoming, friendly and good-natured, interested in others, easy-going, calm and unflustered, or are they reserved, cold and unfriendly, self-absorbed, bad-tempered, with a tendency to over-react? Or some other combination of features?

Personality is generally thought to be 'hardwired' into our brains, either because it involves characteristics we are born with or that we acquire very young and are unable to change substantially. It is best thought of as being that blend of personal characteristics that shape our behaviour and make us an individual; it is that which makes someone psychologically (as opposed to physically) distinct as an individual, which would make you say, 'Oh, that's typical of him/her'.

The 'big five' personality dimensions

These days, psychologists talk about the 'big five' personality traits, as these seem to be the main characteristics that distinguish people and influence their behaviour. The big five are:

- *Neuroticism*: how easily we respond to the world around us – our emotional stability. Some people get upset or angry very easily, others are very stable and, at the extreme, are unresponsive to the world about them.

- *Extraversion*: how much people enjoy being with other people and being actively engaged with them or how much they prefer to be on their own or with small intimate groups (introverts).

- *Openness* to different interests: people with a high level of openness will do lots of things and be very inquisitive, but not examine things in as much depth as people with a low openness who will be highly involved with few interests.

- *Agreeableness*: how accommodating we are to alternative attitudes, values and points of view. People who are most accommodating will accept a wide range, whereas those who are least accommodating will tend to have strong opinions and not listen to others.

- *Conscientiousness*: how committed and organized we are to do something. People who are very conscientious will get on and do what they say they are going to do, whereas people who are not conscientious can be unreliable.

Key ideas

Psychometric tests

Many organizations use psychometric tests as part of their recruitment and development of employees. These tests range from tests of intelligence to tests of personality and motivation.

The most commonly used tests of personality (such as MBTI(™)) still tend to focus on four personality dimensions, rather than five. The dimension not covered by these tests is that concerned with emotional stability (neuroticism). Given that there is still no consensus among the psychological community as to what personality is, let alone how it can be measured, this variation in approaches is not surprising. The best way to deal with any such tests is ask: 'Does this help me to be a better leader?' If it does, use the results, but with due caution, because they may not catch all aspects of your personality.

Personality varies along these five dimensions (you are not *either* extroverted *or* introverted but probably lie somewhere in between the two extremes), and most people will tend to lie towards the middle of the range (Figure 3.1).

This pattern is true for all five traits:

- Extrovert–Introvert
- Neurotic–Stable
- Open–Closed (to new interests)
- Agreeable–Antagonistic
- Conscientious–Unreliable.

It is also worth emphasizing that there is also no clear correlation between the traits – people who are extroverts are not necessarily open to new ideas, for example, but nor are they necessarily closed to them either. One of the reasons that these particular dimensions were selected was because they seemed independent of each other.

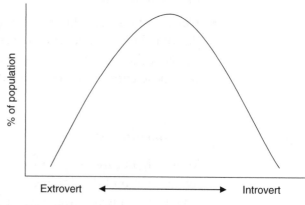

Figure 3.1   Distribution of personality traits

Where two or more traits seemed to be dependent on each other they were combined together, to create the 'big five'.

Reflection

If you were trying to describe your own image of an 'ideal leader', would you expect someone to have any particular personality traits. Where would you want your ideal leader to lie along these five dimensions – in the middle of any, or towards one or other extremes, or could they lie across a wide range of any dimension?

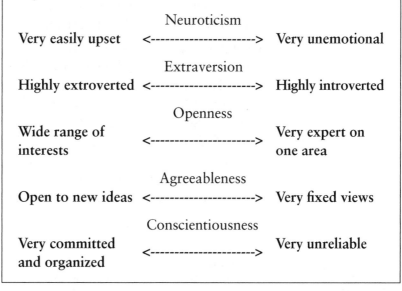

The ideal leader's personality

So what are the most appropriate personality traits for leaders? It is important to emphasize that there are no right answers to this question. Given that there is no great certainty over what personality is, what the dimensions of personality are, or how they are best measured, it would be foolish for anyone to say that: 'The best leaders have this kind of personality mix...'. What is probably true is that people who lie at any of the extremes are likely to have problems as leaders. In the treatment of people who are classed as having 'personality disorders', this usually means that they lie at one extreme on one of these dimensions.

People who are very neurotic will be emotionally very unstable and have difficulty living normal lives but, equally, people who show no emotion at all will have severe problems interacting in society. Extreme extroverts could be exhibitionists; severe introverts could lock themselves away from human company. Extremely open-to-ideas people will always be doing something new, never mastering anything; extreme specialists could be very useful but only in very limited areas. Very 'agreeable' people agree with everyone; their extreme opposites will never change their minds about anything. The most conscientious will not move on until every 't' is crossed and 'i' dotted, no matter how irrelevant; the most unreliable will never do what they say they will do. In other words, to be a leader, people probably need to be only moderately strong or around the middle range of any dimension, and a good case could be made for any particular personality trait (Figure 3.2).

What this suggests is that leaders can come in all shapes and sizes – as you saw in Chapter 1, different leadership styles fit different situations. The same could well be true for leadership personalities – different leaders adopt different ways of working, and what works for one person may not work for another. It is possible that certain types of leadership role require particular personalities, but that does not mean that what works in one place, in one organization and with one group of people will work everywhere. The challenge to anybody in a leadership position is to be aware of their personal

Neuroticism	
Someone who gets enthused and excited about ideas, shows their emotions so that followers know how they feel	Someone who can control their emotions quite well, not get over-excited, and make rational decisions
Extraversion	
Someone who is good with people, able to get on well and show an interest in the people being led	Someone who is able to be a bit detached from the team, not trying to be one of the crowd, and able to earn respect
Openness	
Someone with broad interests, who knows about all aspects of the work being done by the people being led	Very knowledgeable about the technical aspects of the job, seen as an expert by those being led
Agreeableness	
Someone who is willing to listen to others and change own views in the light of discussions	Someone who is clear in own ideas and beliefs, does not flit from one to another to follow what others say
Conscientiousness	
Someone who is focused, gets the job done and does not leave loose ends untied	Someone who is able to generate ideas and get things rolling, delegates responsibility for detail to others

Figure 3.2   Personality traits and leaders

characteristics (including their personality traits) and work to their strengths, while being alert to their weaknesses.

Reflection

One very popular psychometric test was devised by Dr T. Meredith Belbin, called the Team Role Inventory. This is based on Belbin's research into what made effective teams. He was working with management trainees and the teams they were in were engaged in project-type work, so his conclusions are not necessarily applicable to all kinds of teamworking. However, the test he devised focused on aspects of personality and from the results he identified nine different roles. The key feature of his work was that the best teams (in completing the tasks) had a mix of people strong in each of the roles. There was no 'one-size, fits-all'.

Why should it not be the same for leadership? Different personalities will lead in different ways and could it not be the case that these may well work differently with different groups of people?

Attitudes, motivation and emotional intelligence

Chapter 2 looked in some detail at the ethical dimension of leadership ('doing the right thing') and argued that characteristics like honesty, integrity, equity and fairness in the way that leaders behave are important features of effective leadership. As you have seen in this chapter, there is no clear evidence that any one combination of personality characteristics is more likely to make you an effective leader, but that extremes of personality may well prevent you from performing well in the role. Now we will explore a further aspect of people's characters, their attitudes, motivations and emotions.

Leadership attitudes

Attitudes are our positive, neutral or negative views about:

- a particular person
- a group or category of people (racial or religious groups, police officers, etc.)

- types of behaviour (public drunkenness, arguing, etc.) or
- events (the theatre, TV reality shows, etc.).

People are not always clear about their attitudes; they may feel both positive and negative attitudes towards something or someone (*ambivalence*, or what is often called a 'love/hate relationship'); they may also not consciously be aware of how they feel (*implicit*, as opposed to *explicit attitudes*), so that what they say does not reveal their true attitude. Both ambivalence and the existence of implicit as well as explicit attitudes can often cause real confusion, in people themselves and in those they live and work with. The existence of conflicting attitudes is one reason that people experience something called *cognitive dissonance* – when two sets of thoughts ('cognitions') do not fit together logically ('dissonance').

Key idea

> ### Cognitive dissonance
>
> Cognitive dissonance was first identified by psychologist Leon Festinger in the 1950s. He concluded that people will convince themselves that they are telling the truth when required to accept something that they know is not true. The competing ideas (what they are being asked to do and what they know to be the case) cause dissonance – they do not fit together. To resolve this they will look for something that may justify the choice they have to make. Managers required to tell their teams something they believe to be untrue, will find a reason for doing so (it's 'for the good of the company') that enables them to believe the untruth.

It is not too difficult to see that effective leaders, if they are to behave with honesty, integrity, equity and fairness, need to make sure that their attitudes are in line with the principles that govern modern society. People who dislike certain individuals, groups, types of behaviour or events, need to ask themselves if this is appropriate, is it in line with what the society they are part of and the organization they work for would regard as legitimate? For example, people who appear to view members of the opposite sex only in terms of their sexual attraction or physical attributes, express racially intolerant views or who dislike supporters of a particular football team, would not be effective leaders. Their prejudices, apart from being illegal in some cases, would only encourage people with the same prejudices to follow them.

This does not mean that leaders must all fit into the same mould or must be 'politically correct'. There is real room for variation in how leaders behave and the attitudes they hold, so long as their attitudes do not cause them to lie or cheat, treat people unfairly, or show favouritism or prejudice.

Leadership motivation

What motivates a person to perform effectively as a leader? Are they motivated differently from those they lead, or is their motivation the same as effective performers in any role? Before answering these questions, let us just look, quickly, at what is meant by motivation and at some theories of motivation that might help arrive at better-informed answers.

Motivation is the driving force behind our behaviour. It is that psychological or physiological force acting on us that causes us to do something. If we have decided to buy a house and need to increase our income we might be driven to seek a better paid job – a psychological driver. If it is a very hot day and we have been very active, we will become dehydrated and thirsty, seeking refreshment – a physiological driver. Of course, it is not always as easy as that. Behaving in ways that make us attractive to a person to whom we are attracted may appear psychological but could, in fact, be driven by a physiological sex drive.

One of the most straightforward ways of understanding how motivation works was put forward by US psychology professor Abraham Maslow. His *hierarchy of needs* suggests that we have five major drivers that shape our behaviour and that these are arranged in levels (a hierarchy), with the lower ones needing to be satisfied before we move on to the higher ones (Figure 3.3)[1].

It is quite possible that leaders could be personally driven by any of these motivations, depending on the circumstances, but which would drive them to lead others? You may be dying of thirst and seek water, but why lead others in the search, especially if that may mean there is less water to go round? It could be that people who particularly want to lead others are those who are driven by a strong need for self-esteem, especially to be recognized by others.

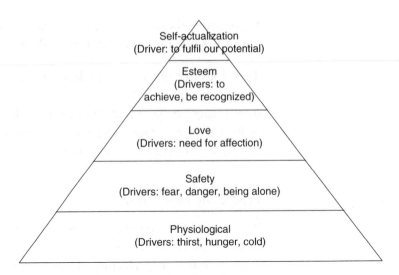

Figure 3.3 Maslow's hierarchy of needs

Another widely known theory (developed by Frederick Herzberg, in his 1959 book *The Motivation to Work*) suggests that we have certain drivers that need to exist to prevent us being dissatisfied (which he called *hygiene* factors) and that these are different from the drivers which actually motivate us (Figure 3.4).

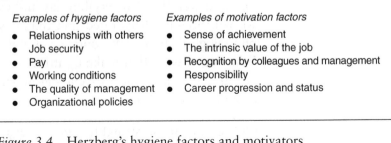

Figure 3.4 Herzberg's hygiene factors and motivators

It is possible to see how some of Herzberg's motivation factors might encourage someone to be a leader – the sense of achieving something, the recognition, responsibility and career progression. Again, as with Maslow, the key issue is, are some of these drivers stronger with some people than others – do they feel a greater need to achieve satisfaction of these motivators?

One final theory about motivation may offer some clues as to what makes leaders 'tick'. Developed by British psychologist Michael Apter, *reversal theory* focuses on how people might be motivated to behave as leaders and suggests that this may be affected by their personality. In other words, different people may be motivated in

Figure 3.5   Reversal theory's motivational states

different ways because of the kind of person they are. According to reversal theory, we are constantly being motivated along four dimensions, each of which contains a pair of states. We will be in one or other of each pair at any one time – there is no intermediary position between the two. The four pairs are illustrated in Figure 3.5.

The key to understanding reversal theory is to think that people can switch between the opposite pairs of states, but that they tend to prefer one to another. To be successful as a leader means that a person can recognize which state might be more appropriate and learn how to get themselves into that motivational state in order to drive their behaviour.

Reflection

Do you recognize these states? Here are some characteristics of each of the four pairs of motivational states. Read each one and ask yourself:

● When do I feel like this?

● What kind of activity should I be in that would benefit from being driven in this way?

Serious	*Playful*
Planning, focusing on achievement and outcomes, avoiding risk and anxiety	Spontaneous and experimenting, adventurous, very much focusing on the here and now

Conforming Compliant and following the rules, fitting in with the group	*Rebellious* Breaking the rules, being innovative, focusing on change and being different
Mastery Focusing on power and control, being tough-minded and in charge	*Sympathy* Being caring and supportive, sensitive to others, giving and receiving affection
Self-oriented Focusing on your own feelings, having a sense of autonomy and concentrating on own needs	*Other-oriented* Empathizing with others, identifying with their feelings, concerned with how your actions affect others

What reversal theory suggests is that we need to match our motivational state (what is driving our behaviour) to the particular circumstances. Being *playful* and *rebellious*, *sympathetic* and *other-oriented* is highly inappropriate when you are trying to clear people away from a spillage of hazardous waste, but may be the most appropriate state when you are trying to encourage a group to come up with innovative new ways of working. One of the useful features of reversal theory is that it argues that, if we can recognize our motivational state, we can assess whether or not it is appropriate for the situation and use techniques like *anchoring* and *triggers* to help us change if we need to.

Key ideas

Anchoring and triggers

Anchoring is a simple technique that anyone can use to help them get themselves into an appropriate motivational state. It is based on two things:

- Recognizing what state you are currently in
- Recognizing what state you should be in.

Then, by thinking of a time and place where we were in the desired state and imagining ourselves back in that time and space, we can recapture the desired state of mind. *Triggers* are physical items that help us to recall the time and place, just as we look back through photo albums to remember a holiday.

Whichever of these theories about motivation seems to make most sense to you, you should ask yourself, 'What drives me to be a leader? What state of mind do I need to be in to encourage people to follow my lead?' Recognizing what drives you is an important step in using your motivation to help you lead people more effectively. What you should be particularly alert to is the desire to acquire power for its own sake, to get pleasure from the ability to control others, or to seek the esteem of others. Leadership is about achieving goals, not a goal in its own right.

Reflection

A good way to think about what you want out of being a leader is to reflect on these words by the Chinese Taoist philosopher Lao Tsu:

To lead people, walk beside them ... As for the best leaders, the people do not notice their existence. The next best, the people honour and praise. The next, the people fear; and the next, the people hate ... When the best leader's work is done the people say, 'We did it ourselves!'

Emotional intelligence

Emotions are the feelings that we get in different situations, which are largely outside our direct control, in response to the world around us. They include our body's physiological response (such as an adrenalin rush caused by fear or a muscle spasm that creates a genuine smile) as well as our psychological reactions (the unprompted thoughts that run through our heads). Some of the many different emotions are listed in Figure 3.6.

Most people will have felt most of these emotions at some stage of their lives. There are a few people who are so lacking in emotional

Amusement	Courage	Friendship	Hate	Patience	Sorrow
Anger	Disgust	Grief	Hope	Rage	Surprise
Anticipation	Desire	Guilt	Joy	Remorse	Terror
Calmness	Envy	Glee	Jealousy	Sadness	
Confidence	Fear	Gladness	Love	Shame	

Figure 3.6   Some of the many emotions

response to the world around them that they feel very few of these emotions, but they are the exception. Some people are very much less emotional than others; some are exceptionally emotional – that is the effect of the personality trait called neuroticism. It is probable that a severe lack of emotional response will prevent people from being effective leaders – they will be felt to be cold and distant and unable to create a willingness to follow. Very emotional leaders, switching from one emotional state to another, are also less likely to be regarded as effective leaders as they will be seen as too unpredictable and disturbing, leading their followers on an emotional switchback ride.

Effective leaders are likely to be seen by those they lead to have 'appropriate' emotions for the situation they face. *Calmness* when the situation is unpredictable, *glee* when the team succeeds at a difficult task, *patience* when a person is struggling to acquire a complex skill, *remorse* at not living up to the high standards that the leader aspires to. The ability to recognize one's own and others' emotional states, and to judge what is the appropriate emotional state to be in, is what is meant by *emotional intelligence*.

First developed as a coherent idea in the early 1990s, by American psychologists John Mayer and Peter Salovey, who suggested that emotional intelligence is how we:

- perceive and identify emotions in ourselves and others
- use emotions to facilitate thought
- understand emotions in others, and
- manage our own emotions.

Leadership is as much an appeal to the emotions as it is to the rational brain. We want people to trust us and believe in us, in order that they will follow us. We can best do this by:

- developing a coherent sense of direction
- recognizing the risks and uncertainties that need to be overcome
- being ethical in our dealings with others and having a coherent set of values that we live by
- being well motivated and able to adjust to the needs of the particular situation
- having a personality that enables us to behave with a degree of emotional stability, neither overwhelming others nor shutting

Self-awareness & understanding

- Awareness and acknowledgement of own body language 'signals' and associated emotions
- Understanding own emotions – listening to and reflecting on intuitive feelings (gut reactions)

Awareness & understanding of others

- Being interested in and aware of others' body language and behaviours
- Interpreting and anticipating others' emotions within the overall context of the situation

Reflection

Reflection on:

- an ethical framework of principles and values
- the overall situational context including own and others' circumstances
- own emotions and others' anticipated emotions
- a communication protocol that will:
    ⇨ demonstrate recognition and understanding of the context
    ⇨ be clearly and appropriately communicated
    ⇨ be genuine, open and honest
    ⇨ show an appropriate degree of warmth

EQ Application

Responding with behaviour that reflects:

- recognition of own and others' emotions
- a match with ethical principles and values
- a relevant communication protocol

Figure 3.7   The EQ4U Process Model

ourselves away, show an interest in new ideas without being superficial, develop expertise without being too narrowly specialized, and ensure that tasks get done without being obsessional.

All of these features of the effective leader involve emotions, both in the leader and the followers. There is a simple technique we can use to be able to recognize and use emotions in order to be able to perform more effectively (to be more emotionally intelligent, in other words). Called the EQ4U Process Model (Figure 3.7)[2], it encourages you to stop before acting and consider your own and others' emotional state, reflect on this and identify the behaviour that is appropriate to bring about the sort of outcome needed. By thinking about their emotions before acting in ways that are driven by them, leaders can reduce the chance of conflict and poor performance.

A key element of emotional intelligence is our ability to read other people's emotions and to recognize how we signal our own emotions through our communications. This highlights the significance of high level communication skills for all leaders, something we will look at in Chapter 4.

Summary

There is no such thing as an ideal set of leadership characteristics. What this chapter shows is that:

- Some extremes of personality may prevent someone from being an effective leader, but that a wide range of personality types are likely to be appropriate, depending on the people being led and the organization in which the leadership occurs.

- Leaders need attitudes towards people and events that are in line with the norms of the society they are part of, and encourage the kind of ethical behaviour associated with effective leaders (honesty, integrity, equity and fairness).

- Leaders should try to understand the motivational drivers that shape their behaviour and be clear that they are appropriate for the role and the task that they face.

- Leaders should be aware of their own and others' emotions and behave in ways that ensures that they encourage the kind of emotional response in others that will produce the desired outcomes.

Notes

1 Maslow's original 1943 paper *A Theory of Human Motivation*, in which he described the hierarchy, is available online at http://psychclassics.yorku.ca/Maslow/motivation.htm and is worth reading as it is not very long and very straightforward.
2 The EQ4U Process Model is taken from the book *Mindchange* by Jan Childs and David Pardey, published by Management Books in 2005.

INTRODUCING LEADERSHIP

4　Leadership skills

In Chapter 3 we looked at personality, attitudes, motivation and emotional intelligence and, in each case, we focused on their significance for effective leaders. Although there is strong evidence to suggest that our personality is pretty well fixed, it interacts with our attitudes, motivation and emotions to shape our behaviour, and there are several practical (how we act) and cognitive (how we think) skills that we can develop and improve to make us effective leaders.

In this chapter we will look at five main sets of skills:

- communication skills
- planning and organizing skills
- personal management skills
- thinking and learning skills
- decision-making skills.

This is not to say these are the only skills that leaders need. Later in the book we will look at other skills that you need in order to undertake specific tasks (such as problem solving or decision-making) and we will develop some of these skills further. But these five skill areas are critical for all leaders in order to shape how they apply their ethical standards, make the most of their personality characteristics, be aware of their own and others' attitudes, channel their motivation and employ their emotional intelligence.

Communication skills

What do we mean by communication? Essentially, it is the ability to transmit a message from one person to another. The message can be:

- information ('There is the spanner')
- an idea or concept ('*Kaizen* is the improvement of a product or process in incremental stages')
- a feeling or emotion ('I hate you').

We communicate with words, with images, with our tone of voice and with our bodies. The basic model of communication, which has been around since the late 1940s, was developed by two engineers, Claude Shannon and Warren Weaver, who worked for the *Bell Telephone Company* in the USA. They were concerned with the process of communicating by voice over the telephone system (not surprisingly) and some of the problems people might experience. Their model (called the *transmission model of communication*) was based on there being:

1 A *source*, which produces a message.

2 A *transmitter*, which encodes the message into signals

3 A *channel*, through which signals are transmitted

4 A *receiver*, which 'decodes' (reconstructs) the message from the signal

5 A *destination*, where the message arrives.

As well as these five, there is a sixth element, *noise*, which can prevent effective communication by distorting the message in transit. There are three possible types of communication problem that noise can produce and which need to be watched for:

• *Technical* problems – how accurately can the message be transmitted?

• *Semantic* problems – how precisely is the meaning conveyed?

• *Effectiveness* problems – how effectively does the message affect behaviour?

Technical problems are not just problems with a bad telephone line, they are also problems to do with how people feel about the person sending the message and its contents, their personality, attitude, motivation and emotional state at the time. Semantic problems arise from not being clear about what you mean, because of the words that you use, the medium you choose to transmit them or the way that you speak or behave. And, even if the message gets through clearly and is understood, if people do not do anything or do not do what they know you want them to do, the communication has failed!

A Finnish academic, called Osmo Wiio, has produced four tongue-in-cheek rules about communication. They are that:

1 If communication can fail, it will.

2 If a message can be understood in different ways, it will be understood in just that way which does the most harm.

Think back to a situation where your message has been misunderstood or not acted on in the way that you wanted. Identify:

- The message you wanted to send
- The channel you used (speaking face to face or by 'phone, by letter or e-mail, etc.)
- The message that appeared to have been received
- The kind of problem that appeared to have occurred (*technical*, *semantic* or *effectiveness*)
- Where or how the problem occurred (the source of *noise*)

3 There is always somebody who knows better than you what you meant by your message.

4 The more communication there is, the more difficult it is for communication to succeed.

If you have not experienced any of these problems, then you are either a highly effective communicator or very lucky!

Sending messages

Bearing Wiio's rules in mind, let us look at how we physically communicate and how this affects the message and how well it is understood, and why communication can fail.

The most significant feature of communication is, of course, the words we use, either in writing or in speech. There are so many ways of saying the same thing that our choice of words conveys a hidden message as well as the surface message that the words appear to be saying. Look at the three sentences in Figure 4.1, each of which is simple guidance on where someone sits.

Words	Message
'Don't sit there, sit here'	'I'm in charge and will decide where you sit'
'Please, sit over there'	'I'm concerned about your comfort'
'Let's sit over here'	'I want to be friendly'

Figure 4.1 Words and meanings

That is just the words – let us see what happens, in Figure 4.2, if you keep the message the same but change channels. Consider the message 'We make the highest quality widgets on the market'; what happens if you send it by the following channels?

Channel	Message
Face to face, to a team member, standing up close and said very sternly	Sounds very much like the team member is in trouble – this could be the start of a severe reprimand
By e-mail to all team members	Let's celebrate, we've just come top in an industry survey!
By letter, to a customer	Do you want the best or the cheapest?

Figure 4.2   Changing channels

The channel and the context in which the words appear change the meaning quite significantly. For a first line or middle manager and leader the most important medium is always going to be face to face with the people you lead. This means that the channel is your voice, and that brings in some quite complex issues of communication.

Key ideas

Oral, verbal and non-verbal communication

People often confuse the two words 'oral' and 'verbal'. *Oral* means with our voice, *verbal* means with words, so writing and speaking are both forms of verbal communication. *Non-verbal* communication refers to the communication that occurs without using words, such as by our tone of voice. *Visual* communication is non-verbal communication which relies on our eyes, which can include written words but is usually used to refer to pictures and symbols, like road signs.

When you communicate orally you will send your message through the words you use, by the way you say them (your tone of voice) and by the way you behave as you speak, what is called your body language or non-verbal communication. These three combine to send your message. In the 1960s, an American psychologist, Albert Mehrabian, studied oral, face-to-face communication (so it does not apply to telephone conversations or written communication, obviously) and discovered in his research that only 7 per cent of the message that recipients received was sent by the words. Thirty-eight per cent was in the tone of voice of the speaker and 55 per cent was through their body language. In other words, it is not what you say but how you say it that counts.

Be careful with these data. The research was very specific and may not be applicable to all communication situations or even to different cultures. However, it is worth examining the two major channels that Mehrabian identified, tone of voice and body language. Your *tone of voice* is literally the emotion or mood that you express through your voice, its rhythm, pitch (high or low) and loudness. Is it happy or sad, commanding or pleading, angry or excited? You can soon tell how other people feel when you hear them speak, so you need to think what message you want your voice to send. For example, in almost every culture people speak in a higher pitch to children and friends, and a lower pitch to be threatening or aggressive.

Reading our bodies

Body language – or *non-verbal communication* – is our ability to send messages by our eye contact, facial expressions, posture and gestures, or proximity. Each of these can have an impact on the people we are communicating with (Figure 4.3).

In the last chapter we introduced the EQ4U Process Model, which finished by recommending 'a relevant communication protocol'. If you wondered what that meant, it is that you should think carefully about all aspects of your communication – your words, your non-verbal behaviour and your channel – to ensure that the full meaning of your message is sent and understood, both *technically* (i.e. people actually receive it) and *semantically* (they 'decode' it accurately), and that they then act on it in the way that you intended (it is *effective*).

Listening actively

A key part of communicating is the receiving of information, just as much as giving it. Active listening means thinking about:

- what is being said
- how it is being said
- why it is being said

65

Body language	Effect
• *Eye contact*	We don't trust people who don't look us in the eye; on the other hand, if someone maintains eye contact for more than about 3 seconds we will start to feel very uncomfortable. Lovers can do it, and people in positions of power who want to dominate others. The best communicators look at individuals in a group constantly, making and breaking eye contact all the time. This means 'I am talking to you, but not threatening or seducing you'! Face to face, they look at someone's face rather than their eyes, only making direct eye contact to emphasize points.
• *Facial expressions*	We can do so much with our faces – grin, grimace, purse our lips or sneer; frown or raise our eyebrows; flare our nostrils; widen or narrow our eyes. Each sends out its own signal, and we can do it intentionally, to emphasize our meaning or without thinking when our emotions take over.
• *Posture and gestures*	How we sit or stand or use our arms can also say so much – standing up straight (formal) or sitting on the corner of a desk (informal); pointing or holding our arms out wide, leaning forward to emphasize the importance, or leaning back to show we are not involved. Crossing arms is often taken to be defensive and even to indicate that someone may be lying – it is also a sign that someone is wanting to feel comfortable and rest their arms!
• *Proximity*	How close or far away we stand or sit also sends out a signal – according to anthropologist Edward Hall, in his 1959 book *The Silent Language*, we recognize four bodily distances • intimate (0–1.5 ft/0.5 m) for the closest friends and intimates • personal-casual (1.5–4 ft/0.5–1.2 m) for people we know casually • social-consultative (4–10 ft/1.2–3 m) routine social interactions with acquaintances as well as strangers, particularly at work • public (10 ft/3 m and beyond) for impersonal and relatively anonymous communication. Leaders who want to assert their power over others will invade their intimate space; those who feel uncomfortable and lack confidence will often maintain the distance of public space.

Figure 4.3   Using non-verbal communication

as you hear it being said. Most people are passive listeners, they listen with only part of their mind as they think about what they want to say. Mainly they are looking for opportunities to break in with their own ideas. To improve your listening skills, try to focus on the person speaking with all your attention and confirm your understanding by *reflecting back* what has been said. 'Reflection' means summarizing the key points of the message you have received, ideally in the form of a question:

• 'Are you asking me to ...?'

or to show your own perceptions of the true message:

• 'I think what you really want me to do is ...'

Sometimes you might feel that what a person has had to say could be said more positively, or what they have said shows that they have missed a significant point. Instead of simply reflecting back what they have said, you could try *reframing* it, putting a different slant on it. For example, suppose that one of the people you lead has just completed a training programme and has taken a very negative view, because the equipment they had learned how to use was not going to be installed for another two months:

- 'It's all very well training me how to use it when it's not actually available. The Manchester people are all getting trained in the week before it's installed.'

Reframing this, you could say:

- 'So we've been chosen to be trained first? They must assume that we will all be capable of remembering what we've learned after two months, rather than needing to be trained immediately before using the equipment.'

Active listening means hearing the message behind the words (in this case, disappointment at not being able to use new learning) and turning it into something positive to remotivate the employee. Leadership demands high levels of communication skills coupled with sensitivity to other people's emotional state, as we saw in Chapter 3.

Planning and organizing

Leaders need to be able to set a direction, work out a route, and make sure that people are able to follow them. This means that they are able to plan and organize effectively.

Let us start by looking at what we mean by *direction*; direction and destination are not the same thing, although they are clearly related. Imagine you are in Edinburgh, Belfast, Cardiff or London, and want to head for (respectively) Glasgow, Omagh, Swansea or Bristol – these are your destinations. Your direction, assuming you do not mind swimming across Lough Neagh, would be (roughly) westwards in each case. In other words, you can head in the same direction but, depending where you start, you arrive in very different places. What is also important to recognize is that you can keep on going westwards (and head in the same direction), but you will leave your destination behind as you do so.

What has this got to do with leadership? Because it helps to make a useful distinction between a manager and a leader. Managers tend to be concerned with destinations – how do we get from here to there. They will be looking at the distance to be travelled, the routes available, and the timescales they need to work to. Managers need to use tools like Gantt charts, Critical Path Method and SMART objectives. Leaders are more concerned with direction – which way are we headed, and why. Direction has no clear end point, so leaders need to be looking further ahead to see barriers that will affect their journey and watch for deviations in the journey that take them off course. All too often, small deviations in the early stages of the journey can lead to the destination being missed further on the journey.

The role of managers is to try to make sense out of uncertainty, to set clear destinations and work out how to reach them. The role of leaders is to recognize that uncertainty is a fact of life, that the world is naturally chaotic and that if things can go wrong they usually will go wrong. By focusing on where the organization and the team are headed, and understanding why they are headed that way, the leader pays less attention to destinations and more to the direction. Whereas the manager focuses on objectives and targets, the leader is concerned with *mission* and *values*.

- A mission statement is a way of setting direction, to say what you (your organization, department or team) want to be, whom you want to serve and what drives you.
- A values statement spells out the drivers and the beliefs underpinning them in more detail.

The best way to develop a mission statement is to work with the people you lead (or a representative group – no more than 8 or 9) and to ask: 'What do we really believe in (as a team, department or unit), that should guide our work practices?' This is how you define your *values*. Values are the principles that guide how you should all behave and interact with other people. They help you to define what is right and what is wrong.

A sales office might decide that its values include:

- Helping colleagues and customers as much as possible
- Being honest and accurate in dealings with colleagues and customers
- Using resources sparingly and appropriately.

Reflection

The best illustration of what a mission statement should do was the quality policy quoted by the great US quality guru, JM Juran, in the first edition of his massive *Quality Control Handbook*:

'We will build good ships, at a profit if we can, at a loss if we must, but always good ships' (*Newport News Shipbuilding and Dry Dock Company* now operating as *Northrop Grumman Newport News*)

How well do you think this works as a mission statement? It is easy to criticize (What does 'good' mean? How long could they trade at a loss?), but it captures the values underpinning the organization, a deeply felt commitment to quality.

From this, they could develop a mission statement that would help to inspire them to live by these values, such as:

To provide a helpful, friendly and efficient service to customers and colleagues to ensure orders are processed and despatched quickly and accurately.

A good mission statement is one that you can put up the wall, in large letters, without feeling embarrassed. Unlike (SMART) objectives, that enable a manager to judge progress and performance, values and mission statements are not measurable or achievable. That does not stop people being committed to them, being inspired by them and using them to guide their performance.

Does that mean that by becoming a leader you should abandon managerial practices of objectives and measuring progress and performance? No, because, as a leader *and* manager, you have to fulfil both roles. Your job is to inspire people to work to the values you have agreed and to head in the direction set by the mission statement (leadership), and to achieve the objectives and operational standards by which performance is measured (management). If you do the first part well – leadership – the second part is so much easier and the levels achieved so much higher. Leadership and management complement each other, they do not replace each other.

LEADERSHIP SKILLS

Personal management skills

A leader leads by example. A good leader sets a standard that others can measure themselves by. This does not mean that they must always try to be better than the people they lead, because many leaders will have followers who are technically better than they are at specific tasks. What it does mean is that they set the standard for living up to the values that they – and the people they lead – espouse. If you want your team to be honest, show integrity, treat people equitably and fairly, then you must do so yourself. And, when you fail in any of these respects, admit it and make clear that you will try harder next time.

People do not expect their leaders to be foolproof – in fact, a leader who aspires to perfection is only preparing for failure. What they do look for is honesty, integrity and fairness, because through them comes *trust*. Trust is a magic word in leadership because it is the hardest thing to acquire and the easiest to lose. Every decision you make, every act you perform has the potential to add a little to the trust people feel for you – and to destroy it completely. If you are honest 99 times out of a hundred, the one lie destroys all the trust built up on the 99 other occasions. This is why personal management is so important.

What do we mean by personal management? Personal management is the awareness of your own strengths and weaknesses as a person; not your job-related skills specifically, but your personality, values, emotions and how they express themselves in your relations with others. This is why psychometric tests are so valuable, because good ones help you to gain an insight into your own personality and other characteristics. Although you may not be able to do much to change many of these, at least in the short term, you can recognize them and take steps to compensate.

- If you are intolerant of people who seem a little too superficial and uncommitted to their work, ask yourself: 'Is their standard of work lower than others', or is it just their personality that I don't like?'. Try to separate your feelings from your objective analysis of others.

- If you find it difficult to discuss your feelings with others, say so, and look for opportunities where you feel safe to speak about just one thing you feel particularly strongly about, so that you can develop your confidence.

- If you find the pace of change is too fast, and that you do not have time to master new skills and tasks as fully as you would like, then ask yourself: 'Which aspects of these skills or tasks are most important? Can I attempt to master just those areas and accept that I can't do everything?'

Reflection

Look back over the explanation of values, personality, attitudes and motivation and ask yourself:

- What are my particular beliefs, personality characteristics, attitudes and motivations that shape my behaviour at work?
- Which of these will help make me a more effective leader?
- Which of these inhibit my performance as a leader?
- What can I do to build on my personal strengths and compensate for my personal weaknesses, to become a better leader?

As well as these personal characteristics that shape your behaviour, there are some specific skills that you should develop, relating to your work role, to be more effective. In particular, you need to be clear about your priorities as a leader and plan your work to reflect that. Leaders are responsible for the well-being and performance of the people they lead, so these are always the most important part of the job. Always make sure there is enough time in your day to check that people are not having problems (personal or task-related). This is often called MBWA – management by walking about – but it is not about being a lurking presence, it is about taking an interest in people and what they are doing. It means being alert to problems and taking action to resolve them, or encouraging others to do so, and going to people rather than expecting them to come to you, which is a mark of respect. That means being able to plan your workload and delegate to others, if appropriate, so that you can spend the time doing the important work of a leader. One of the most useful tools you can use to help you is the urgent/important grid, as this helps you to identify your priorities.

Key idea

The urgent/important grid

The grid uses two main dimensions to judge a task:

- How important is it?
- How urgent is it?

All too often we confuse the two ideas. By allocating tasks to one of the four squares in the grid, you can decide the level of priority you give to each one

	More urgent	*Less urgent*
More important	Do it as soon as you can or delegate to someone who can do it promptly, monitoring closely	Plan when you will do this and organize your work round it
Less important	Do it now, quickly, or delegate to someone who can do it now	If this needs doing get someone else to do it or use it to fill a gap in your workload at an appropriate time

Here are some other tips for managing your workload better, so that you can focus on your role as a leader:

- Keep your desk or workspace clear and tidy, with documents, materials and equipment stored properly

- Prepare 'to do' lists and work schedules, with regular tasks planned and time reserved for their completion

- Do difficult or unpleasant tasks first and leave unimportant tasks, or the ones you enjoy, for later – enjoyable jobs can be the reward for completing the unpleasant ones

- Set aside time for private or undisturbed time (e.g. making 'phone calls) and make it clear that you should only be disturbed for real emergencies – other than that, be approachable at all times

- Try to complete a task once you start it. One technique is to put a tick in the top right hand corner of a document every time you use it. Aim never to put more than three ticks, then no more than two, until you have organized your work so that jobs get done in a planned and organized way, and are not set aside and picked up again later

- Monitor how you use your time, and make clear plans to change behaviour which means that time is not used effectively.

Alongside tools and techniques for managing your own workload is the recognition that a critically important task is to talk to the people you lead about their work and their goals, regularly and openly, seeking to find out what needs to be done to improve their performance and achieve their goals. Managers may have formal performance management or appraisal interviews with their staff every three, six or 12 months. Leaders speak to them every day or so, identifying problems and getting them resolved as quickly as they can. Urgent tasks are often important tasks that were not dealt with early, and relate to problems that could have been resolved easily when they first emerged. Leaders make other people's problems their concern, and get them resolved.

The measure of the effective leader is the ability to judge what is important – not just to you and your line manager, but to the people you lead. Effective leadership is the ability to give others' priorities as much value as you give your own, and those to whom you report. This is what Robert Greenleaf meant when he used the term 'servant-leadership'. Most organization charts show the lines of control going down and the lines of accountability going up. Effective leaders see that the people they lead should control their lives (because if they are not properly cared for, the tasks will not get done). Equally, they see themselves as accountable to those they lead at least as much as they do to those they report to. The lines of control and the lines of accountability go both up and down!

Thinking and learning skills

Can you be a better thinker or learner? Most people assume that their thinking and learning abilities are fixed at birth, by their level of general intelligence. The truth is that thinking and learning both involve skills that you can learn and improve, and that these are not dependent on your level of general intelligence. For a start, what is called 'general intelligence' is just one aspect of our abilities as human beings, and not necessarily the most important one.

Howard Gardner, professor of education at Harvard University, first put forward the idea that we all have multiple intelligences in his 1983 book, *Frames of Mind*. He suggested that the traditional idea of intelligence, the one that IQ tests measure, is far too limited. What about the ability to play a musical instrument (which some people seem to be able to do so easily) or learn foreign languages? What about the ability to dance well, or make complex objects? When a builder sees a complex set of plans and is able to translate that into the physical structure envisaged by the architect, or a craftsperson produces a sculpted steel die to be used in plastic moulding, what 'intelligence' is that?

What Gardner suggests is that there are several different intelligences and that people may be naturally more intelligent in some than in others. Modern societies tend to value certain of these intelligences more than others, but that does not mean that they are intrinsically better. As a leader you need to be aware of what you are good at and what you are less good at (know your own strengths and weaknesses) and make the most of all your abilities. There are very many ways of thinking and making sense of the world around us, and leaders need to develop their skills in using the natural intelligence they were born with.

Learn to think better

Although there is a myriad of tools and techniques you can use to improve your thinking and learning (and we will look at some of these in more detail in the next chapter), you should be aware of the following principles:

- People may not be able to improve their intelligence significantly, but they can improve the way they use it
- People think and learn in different ways, and what works for you may not work for others
- Our capacity to learn is unlimited. Pre-school children learn at least one language (some learn two or even three) so imagine what we can learn as adults
- You continue to learn all your life. Age is no barrier to learning, but nor is youth, the only barrier is the belief that you do not need to or cannot learn.

Effective leaders are always willing to learn, are ready to acknowledge when they do not know or cannot do something, and respect others who will teach them. There are various theories about how we learn, and not all of them are accepted as being wholly valid.

However, here are some useful guidelines to help you think and learn more effectively:

1 People learn by engaging all their senses, by listening to others, by asking questions and discussing ideas and practices, and by engaging in activities. Use all these means to learn and make sense of the world around you – as the Chinese philosopher Confucius said: 'I hear and I forget. I see and I remember. I do and I understand'.

2 When you hear or see something new, be prepared to spend time reflecting, mulling over what you have seen or heard, to make sense of it. Then consciously look for an association with what you already know or can do, as if you were putting it in the appropriate place in a filing cabinet. That way you will be able to recall it better when you need it.

3 When you are trying to make sense of complex issues, break them down and look for ways of simplifying the elements, before reassembling them. A valuable technique is the Mind Map®; used properly, this can help you learn in ways that you had not imagined[1]. Other mechanisms include using flow charts and systems diagrams – there is more about these ideas in Chapters 10 and 11.

4 Always be prepared to ask questions; do not be afraid to reveal your lack of knowledge, because that shows lack of respect for others and a lack of integrity in yourself. Ask questions to help you:

- *clarify meanings*, or what is happening or being done ('What is…?')

- *explore assumptions* about why people believe that something is the case or is happening or should be done that way ('What are you assuming?')

- *probe the reasons* for things happening or evidence to support arguments ('Why does that…? Is there any evidence for that?')

- *investigate people's viewpoint or perspectives* ('What leads you to say that? What are you implying by that?')

- *explore the implications or consequences* ('If we did do that, what would be the effect?').

To be an effective leader you do not need to be more intelligent or more skilled than the people you lead, but you do need to be more ready to think about what is happening and to learn. That way, you will be better able to understand the challenges facing you and make informed decisions about what to do as a result.

Decision-making skills

The definition of leadership we used in Chapter 1 was 'the ability to bring about movement or change in a group or organization, when there is risk or uncertainty, by inspiring others to head in a particular direction'. The significance of this definition in decision-making is that it is far easier to make decisions in periods of calm and certainty, when there is little or no change and the options facing you are limited, and the likely outcomes are predictable. When the world is changing and your organization has to change in response, then the level of risk and uncertainty increases and decisions have to be based on the option that is most likely to produce the desired outcome or that is most in line with your values.

The challenge for leaders is to make decisions when they have only partial information; the US Secretary of Defence, Donald Rumsfeld, described this problem in a way that earned him the Plain English Campaign's *Foot In Mouth* trophy:

...there are things we know we know. We also...know there are some things we do not know. But there are also unknown unknowns – the ones we don't know we don't know.

Although he expressed himself poorly (his words have been edited to make them clearer!), what Rumsfeld said is true. When faced with any decision there are three things we need to be aware of:

1 what we know about the situation
2 what we do not know about the situation
3 what we do not know that we do not know about the situation.

Look at Figure 4.4 and you will get some idea of the way that uncertainty can affect our decision-making ability.

How do we reduce the risk or uncertainty in decision-making? The first step is to collect information, analyse it, structure it and make sense of it. *Analyse* means breaking it down and looking for patterns (which may mean putting data into tables or charts; it might mean seeking common elements in events or documents). *Structure* means reassembling what we have learnt into a coherent picture of the whole. *Making sense* is then about seeing what we can learn

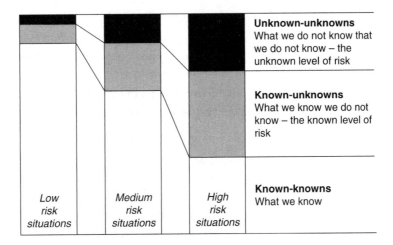

Figure 4.4   Recognizing risk

from the information, and identifying what we know and what we do not know. It is useful to use this three-stage approach because it encourages you to approach decision-making with care.

What you do not know is what determines the level of risk or uncertainty – and because you do not know all of what is missing, you cannot easily assess exactly what the risk is. Let us look at a practical example to see what this means. Assume that you are leading a change project to introduce a new Customer Relationship Management (CRM) system into your organization. This IT-based system manages all aspects of the organization's relationships with customers – sales and promotional planning, order-taking, processing and despatching, invoicing and credit checking. Thirty people will be affected, all of whom need training. Existing systems will be removed, new hardware and software installed. How long will customer management be disrupted and what level of errors and delays will occur during the change process?

- By collecting information about the experience in other similar-sized organizations making the same kind of change and by analysing, structuring and making sense of that information you can know a lot and reveal some of the things you did not realize you knew.

- You know that you do not know how the people in the other organizations felt about the change (their enthusiasm to make the change effective) or whether their starting knowledge and skills were the same as your own organization's, or how their ability to learn compares.

- You do not know what you do not know. Have any of the people in your organization decided to leave but not told you? Have any of your competitors prepared a major sales campaign just as you introduce the new system and will be slow to respond? Are there any technical faults in the software or hardware that the suppliers do not know about or have not told you about?

How do you make the best decisions in this sort of situation? First, by being open and honest about the change, involving as many people as possible to maximize the knowledge and the awareness of the situation, reducing the amount that you 'do not know'. Second, by doing some 'what if' thinking. 'What if' means thinking about all the possible scenarios that could arise and making some educated guesses about the likelihood of their happening. This helps you to move some items from the 'unknown-unknowns' box to the 'known-unknown' box.

Key idea

The wisdom of crowds

Involving others in decision-making is not about spreading responsibility for the decisions – leaders should always accept full personal responsibility for the decisions they make. It is based on a simple principle – groups make better decisions than individuals (although not always as quickly). James Surowiecki[2] argues that groups of people (generally, the larger the better) make better decisions than individuals, so long as the group satisfies four conditions, that:

1 there is diversity of opinion

2 each person's decision is independent of the others

3 people can specialize and draw on their local knowledge

4 the separate views can be drawn together into a single judgement.

Effective leaders should ensure that each person is able to contribute and then draw together the separate views into a collective decision.

There are many tools and techniques you can use to help you and the people you lead to make better decisions, but the most important thing for any leader is to be prepared to make a decision. All too often we put off decisions because the risks and uncertainties seem too great – the known-unknowns and unknown-unknowns overwhelm us! By waiting, we hope to resolve these, but by the time we have reduced the risk and uncertainty to a manageable level, it is too late to make a decision, the opportunity has passed. Effective leaders accept risk and uncertainty, do what they can to reduce it, but are then prepared to stick the head above the parapet and say: 'This is what we should do'. It is useful to ask the question: 'Would making a wrong or poor decision be better or worse than making no decision?' Often the answer is no. A failure to make any decision is the worst possible outcome there could be. It is at times like this that your leadership characteristics are needed:

- Honesty, integrity, equity and fairness, so that you are seen to be doing what you believe is right

- Insights into your own personality, attitudes, motivation and emotions, and the effect that they are having on your decision-making

- The ability to communicate well with others, to involve them, collect information and make your decision clear to them

- Setting a clear direction that you can use to help make a decision with incomplete information, having set a good example to others so that they will trust you to lead them in the right direction, and having the willingness to ask questions, listen and make sense of what you hear, so that you are seen to be making informed decisions and people will support you even if they do not agree with you.

Much of what we look at in the rest of *Introducing Leadership* will develop your knowledge about aspects of leadership where you will need to make decisions, reducing the 'unknowns' but never eliminating them. It is these leadership qualities that will help you to make the decisions that mean that you and those you lead are most likely to be doing the right thing.

Summary

- Leaders need to be aware that communication relies at least as much on how you say things as what you say. By appreciating how easy it is for messages to get distorted and misunderstood, leaders take care to ensure that they communicate effectively, encouraging the behaviour that they intended.

- Leaders also have to be good – active – listeners, so that they recognize the message behind the words others use, confirm it through reflection and, if necessary, alter the emphasis through reframing, to turn negative attitudes into positive ones.

- Managers need to have a clear sense of direction and of the values that guide that direction in order that they can ensure that what is being done is planned and organized to reflect those values and heads in the right direction.

- Leaders need to set an example to others in the way that they work. That means they need personal management skills to organize their own workload, set priorities and delegate work, where appropriate.

- Leaders need to make the best use of their intelligence, not necessarily be more intelligent than others. This means using some simple but effective skills to structure their thinking and learning so that they make informed decisions that are more likely to produce the desired outcomes.

- To make decisions, leaders need to recognize that risk and uncertainty reduce the chance of getting it right, every time, but they do not allow that to prevent them making decisions. Instead, they make an effort to minimize the uncertainty and involve others, to produce better decisions, and then stand by them.

Notes

1 Mind mapping is a technique developed by Tony Buzan. To find out more about it, go to http://www.mind-map.com/EN/index.html
2 The four conditions for group decisions to be better than individual decisions are on page 10 of James Surowiecki's *The Wisdom of Crowds*, published in 2004 by Little, Brown.

5   Developing yourself as a leader

Gerry Randell, Emeritus Professor at Bradford University's School of Management, has described leadership as 'nothing more, nor less, than a magnificent human skill.' But, he went on to say:

Managers who aspire to be called leaders appear to prefer a quick fix, a secret formula or a magic potion. The suggestion that the key lies within themselves and they would have to spend as much time and effort on it as they do learning how to interact with a golf ball or a yacht is not to their liking.

This is the challenge of leadership; it is possible to learn some tools and techniques, and debate different definitions of leadership, but to work on honing your leadership skills is demanding and slow. In this chapter we will look at some of the things that you can do to develop yourself, and also argue that effective leaders never stop wanting to learn and improve, that the desire to be better leaders is an important part of their make up.

How do leaders learn?

Much the same as everyone does, is the simple answer, although there are some aspects of leadership that do require some special learning strategies. We will look at these later, but start with the basics of learning. Essentially, people learn three different types of skills:

- *cognitive skills* – this ranges from knowing facts (Pythagoras' theorem) to applying rules, principles and practices to their knowledge to make judgements or decisions (how to calculate the height of a mountain using Pythagoras' theorem and a theodolite)
- *affective skills* – these are the skills associated with using values to make judgements ('that person is better than me')
- *psycho-motor skills* – these are the skills associated with physical action, from moving objects (e.g. setting up a theodolite) to manipulating the body to communicate (e.g. body language).

Leadership involves all three types of skill, although many people overlook the third type (psycho-motor) because they overlook the significance of non-verbal communication in leadership. Although the three different types of skill are separated out for classification, they are often integrated in use. A leader who is trying to persuade a team member of the need to improve practical performance in a task will use cognitive skills to identify the learning need, affective skills to convince the person and psycho-motor skills in communicating this to the person.

The learning cycle – learning from experience

One of the most commonly used models to explain how people develop their cognitive, affective or psycho-motor skills was developed by American academic, David Kolb. In his 1984 book, *Experiential learning: experience as the source of learning & development*, he outlines a four-stage cycle that enables effective learning to take place. It starts with a *concrete experience* as the basis for learning, and *observation and critical reflection* as the mechanism by which we can make sense of it. From this comes *abstract conceptualization and generalization* (identifying underpinning principles and patterns) followed by *active experimentation and testing our new ideas* to try out other ways of acting, and using those experiences to refine and improve, by further reflection, etc. (see Figure 5.1).

What Kolb argues is that the most effective learning (rather than just learning by rote) happens when people use their own experience as the basis for learning (hence *experiential* learning), but that simply experiencing something does not mean that you have learnt anything. People go through life having the same experiences, day after day, and learn nothing from them. To be of value, we have to make some effort to reflect on what we have learnt,

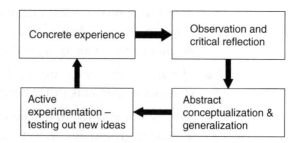

Figure 5.1   The Kolb Experiential Learning Cycle

use this reflection to make sense of the experience and try out other ways of acting.

Reflection

Reflection on experience is not just thinking about or describing events, it involves:

- *analysing* what happened, working out why it happened as it did, identifying the causes and consequences of what happened and considering what alternative behaviour or effects were possible
- *evaluating* what happened to make judgements about the events and your own and others' behaviour, asking yourself if your actions or decisions were the most appropriate, were successful, and the effect they had on others
- drawing *hypotheses* about what else might have happened or been done, or what alternative decisions might have been made
- assessing your *emotional responses*, asking yourself how you felt about the events and how you think others felt about them (using your emotional intelligence).

This is not easy to do well, although you will find it gets easier with practice and with the help of others. You will do it better if you ask the people you work with for feedback and use this to help understand what happened. Feedback is easiest to accept when you feel that you performed well and are asking people to confirm that you did do well and *might just* be able to make some small improvements. It is hardest when things went badly, when you handled the situation completely wrongly, and you feel defensive and embarrassed about it. This is where your true leadership ability comes to the fore. Anybody can accept praise, it takes a true leader to accept responsibility whatever the outcome. Everybody makes mistakes, leaders acknowledge their mistakes, learn from them and move on.

Key ideas

Feedback

Feedback is reaction to any event or behaviour, which may be invited or spontaneous (such as the looks on people's faces, or their other body language). When you invite people to give feedback you should be willing to hear what they say without challenging or arguing with them. Ask people to describe *what they saw* and say *what they felt* about it. Ask questions to explore either but do not try to change their views (that is argument not feedback). Only when they have had a chance to say what they saw and felt should you make any comments, and then only to correct any serious errors about the facts. Acknowledge their right to see things differently from you.

Reflection is easier if you have help, from a manager, colleagues, a coach or mentor who are helping you to develop yourself as a leader. There is more about this a bit further on in this chapter.

Conceptualization – learning the theory

As Gerry Randell argued, leadership is about practical skills, but all good practice is underpinned by an understanding of 'why?' – why some things work and others do not, why people behave as they do, etc. One result of reflection is that you should be left with questions about why things happened, and an effective leader is never content to leave such questions unanswered. Why did he react like that? Why does she want to make those changes? Why is it so hard to get the organization to accept new ideas? The best learning comes from working out answers to these questions yourself, supported by researching well-regarded theory and practice. You can:

- read books[1], academic journals, magazine articles and other printed resources
- research on the Internet (but be very careful over what you find – you may have to kiss a lot of frogs before you find your prince or princess!)
- ask people whose knowledge and experience you respect, inside the organization and through your personal networks (something we deal with later in this chapter)
- attend courses, conferences and seminars
- use flexible learning materials[2] or e-learning.

The process of *abstract conceptualization* is about understanding the principles that underpin behaviour. It is *abstract* because you are moving from the concrete (the specific experience) to the general (the set of all similar occurrences), where the core features of the behaviour are being identified. It is *conceptualization* because it is about concepts or ideas, rather than the individual circumstances. To give you one example, later in *Introducing Leadership* we will look at the different ways that organizations can be structured, and will use something called systems theory as a way of explaining the differences and the effects that they have. Organizations are real (concrete); systems theory is an abstract concept, yet it helps make sense of those concrete structures.

Why do leaders need to learn about abstract concepts? Because they need to understand why certain behaviour produces the effects it does. A child can be enchanted by watching puppets without caring how they work, but a parent can understand that people are pulling their strings and marvel at their skill. Understanding is the first step to being able to pull the strings yourself. Similarly, if a team responded in a particular way, it was not just because their leader did X, but because they had just experienced Y, and there is a theory that says X + Y will produce Z. If their leader does not appreciate this and tries to repeat the event, doing X when the team have just experienced W, the result could be a disaster!

Experiment

The next stage in Kolb's learning cycle is *active experimentation*. This means planning to try things out. In Chapter 4 you learned about body language and the effect that your tone of voice and your body language can have on your ability to communicate effectively. You may well feel that you need to work on improving your communication skills and so you try to change your tone of voice, your eye contact and the way you use your body to improve your communication skills. That involves active experimentation.

There are different ways of trying things out. On training courses you may have the chance to use role-play exercises to practise skills. There may be opportunities outside work to try things out and see what effect they have. You can tell the people you lead that you want to develop certain skills and ask them to bear with you while you do so, and give you feedback on the result (so that you continue round the cycle).

> *Reflection*
>
> How do you feel about trying out new practices? Do you enjoy role-play exercises on courses and are you always happy to do something new (you may well be quite extrovert and open in your personality)? Or does the thought of people watching you fill you with dread, and do you prefer sticking to the tried and trusted ways of doing things?
>
> If you do feel more like the latter, then look for situations where you feel safest (say, a small group you know well) and only try out something simple, but add to it each time you get the opportunity. Often the best change comes from small steps, because that way you can get each element right.

Leadership is about practical skills, and the only way you can develop a practical skill is by practice. Active experimentation is about practice, but practice in a controlled, planned way, something that is much easier if you have help. There are various ways that you can get help to support you and help you become a better leader, such as:

- *coaches*, who can give specific guidance on using skills and discuss performance, helping with reflection and abstract conceptualization
- *mentors*, who are similar to coaches, but provide more of a model of good practice on which to base your behaviour and discuss it with the mentor
- *action learning sets*, in which a group of managers in similar roles collaborate on improving their leadership performance, again helping with the reflection and abstract conceptualization stages.

But the most important support must come from within, from a real desire to change and improve. Whatever external support leaders get, it will only be of value if they have the commitment to learn.

How do people learn?

Kolb's experiential learning cycle describes an ideal, starting with the experience, moving on to reflect on it, developing understanding through abstract conceptualization and then trying out new ways of working in a planned and controlled way. However, people seem to have preferences for different stages of the cycle. Some like the abstract conceptualization stage, and are very well read on ideas about leadership, but cannot put any of it into practice. Others will try out every new idea without a second's hesitation, but never really spend time working out how or why things work. Others will spend hours reflecting on what has happened, examining every second of the experience, but not use that to try out anything different.

Understanding these learning preferences (or *learning styles*) can help leaders to draw on their strengths as learners (good reflector or experimenter with new ideas), while being aware of their weaknesses (not using the reflection to improve performance, or not using new experiences to work out what works and what does not). The best learners work through all stages; the best leaders recognize the importance of learning to improve performance and use their strengths and compensate for their weaknesses to maximize their learning.

The other thing to remember is that skills can only be developed in steps; trying to transform performance completely, in one go, is bound to fail. The most effective learning and skills development comes from focusing on the application of specific skills and improving them bit-by-bit.

Learning styles

There are various assessment tools available to test people's learning styles, their preferences for particular stages of the learning cycle (for example Kolb's own organization, Experience Based Learning Systems, offers an assessment tool called the *Learning Styles Inventory*). These tend to focus on preferences for pairs of adjoining stages on the experiential learning cycle rather than single stages. Many training and development departments use these assessment tools, as do many training providers and colleges, but knowing your learning style is only of value if this is used to improve learning. One of the problems that many people have is to assume that their learning style limits them to learning in only one way. Quite the reverse; knowing your learning style can help in working round the cycle by not getting stuck at one stage (Figure 5.2).

Learning cycle preference	Improving your learning
• Experience and reflection (Kolb has labelled people with this preference as *divergers*)	If you enjoy using your experience to generate new ideas and think about alternative ways of working, you should consider how you might improve your learning by considering how this relates to theories or principles, and how this can inform future behaviour
• Reflection and conceptualization (Kolb has labelled people with this preference as *assimilators*)	If you enjoy seeing how your experience links in with theories and principles, perhaps you need to move on from looking for reasons to consider how that should affect your behaviour
• Concepts and experiments (Kolb has labelled people with this preference as *accommodators*)	If you enjoy trying new things out, but perhaps are less good at exploring the consequences of your actions, try reflecting on what happened and using the results to inform future behaviour
• Experiments and experiences (Kolb has labelled people with this preference as *convergers*)	If you enjoy taking risks, trying things out and adapting your plans to respond to the moment, you could perhaps reflect more, look at what actually happened and explore the reasons why things worked and why they did not

Figure 5.2   Using learning styles to improve your learning

(An alternative assessment tool used widely in the UK, developed by Peter Honey and Alan Mumford, uses the labels *reflector, theorists, pragmatists* and *activists* to describe similar preferences.)

Some people suggest that by knowing your learning style preference you will know how to select appropriate types of learning – if you prefer experiments and experience, focus on that. Although you will probably get a lot out of experiments and experience, you need to be aware that you may fail to take advantage of the opportunity to learn from reflection and conceptualization. What you need to do is to be careful that a preference does not stop you learning effectively. The best learning comes from travelling round the complete cycle – your preference may suggest where you will tend to focus and, if you are not careful, get stuck.

'Modalities' – seeing, hearing and doing

Parallel to the idea that people have certain learning style preferences, focused on areas of the experiential learning cycle, are theories that people prefer learning through particular senses. This idea is called *learning modalities* (because it concentrates on the mode of learning) and is particularly associated with Neuro-Linguistic Programming (or NLP[3]), although it is by no means exclusive to NLP. The modes of learning, and the senses associated with them, that may be dominant, are:

- *visual* (learning by watching and seeing)
- *auditory* (learning by listening and hearing)
- *kinaesthetic* (learning by participating and doing).

There are some doubts about the idea that people have a preference for learning in one way, but there is no doubt that people respond well to having all their senses engaged in learning, and that:

- watching someone do it
- listening to them explain how and why they do something, and
- trying it yourself

is a good way to learn new skills. To improve yourself as a leader, try watching people who exhibit skills that you want to develop (visual). Talk to them about what they do and how they have learnt the skills (auditory), and then try the skills out yourself (kinaesthetic), ideally asking the other person to observe and give feedback. If you find that watching is better for you than talking about how to do it or doing it for yourself, then it may be that you are a visual learner, but that does not mean that you should only watch, anymore than you should allow yourself to concentrate on only one stage in the experiential cycle.

Action Learning

Action Learning is a way of improving your performance that was first developed some 50 years ago, by Professor Reg Revans. Revans worked with managers at the National Coal Board and the National Health Service, before moving to Belgium, where he used Action Learning with many national and international organizations.

Action Learning is not a particularly complex idea; it is based on the principle that most leaders and managers can resolve the problems or challenges that they face with the help of others in the same position plus advice on the best sources of theory and practice. They get this help by working together in groups, called Action Learning (AL) sets, facilitated by set advisors, who are specialists in leadership and management learning. The way that AL sets work is that members take it in turns to present a 'problem', an issue that they face at work that they need help in resolving. Other set members explore the problem with them by asking questions (not giving advice) that enables the problem's causes to be explored and the individual to work out likely solutions. Advisors can point the set to resources (such as books, articles, web pages, training courses or flexible and e-learning) that can help them to make sense of the problem and work out the likely solutions – what Revons labelled *programmed knowledge*. True learning, he said, comes from combining this programmed knowledge with questioning, which he expressed as a simple equation:

L (learning) = P (programmed knowledge) + Q (questioning)

What makes Action Learning so useful is that it concentrates on what someone can do to be more effective in their role. The members of the AL set provide mutual support and, by solving individual problems, help everyone to learn and develop. If you get an opportunity to be a member of an action learning set then you should seize it, as it is likely to prove worthwhile.

Networking

Networking – the active development and maintenance of contacts with a wide range of people – is a very effective developmental approach. You can identify people with the kind of skills you want to develop yourself, to provide models of best practice, allowing you to observe their performance and discuss it with them. It also enables you to increase the range of experiences on which to reflect and develop your understanding of effective leadership.

Networks can include membership of professional bodies (like the Institute of Leadership and Management) and of organizations that aim to bring leaders and managers together socially, often for charitable purposes (Rotarians, Lions, Round Table, Soroptimists, etc.). It can also include informal networks of friends and acquaintances, including colleagues at work, with whom you can discuss and develop your management and leadership ability.

A critical feature of networking is that you get out what you put in. You have to build your own networks (simply joining an organization is not networking, but the chance to meet people with whom to network), by initiating contact, and maintaining it, giving at least as much as taking. If you are not a particularly extrovert person, you may find it challenging to engage in active networking, especially in formal groups, but you should make the effort to build at least a small network of people you feel comfortable with to be able to watch them, listen to them and practise the skills that they possess.

Managing your leadership learning

Right through this chapter, in fact, right through this book, we have argued that leaders need to take responsibility for their own learning. If you cannot lead yourself you will struggle to lead others. That does not mean that leaders have to work on their own, but that they actively take responsibility for their own development and use the resources available to assist them, especially their employer's training and development resources. Developing yourself is no different from developing the people that you lead, a topic we look at further in Chapter 7. It involves three simple questions:

- Where am I now?   What knowledge, skills and experience do I have?

- Where do I want to be?   What kind of leadership behaviour do I want to develop?

- How can I close the gap? What kinds of learning and development activity will help me develop those behaviours?

The following tools and techniques can help you undertake this, but the most significant ingredient is you, and your commitment to personal development.

Where am I now? A personal SWOT

A SWOT analysis (Figure 5.3) is a simple but very useful tool for self-assessment and development planning, enabling you to identify where you are currently.

The first two parts of the SWOT analysis are about you; the last two about your work and personal environment. In assessing your strengths and weaknesses, you should take advantage of as many sources of information as possible. If you have had any form of skills assessment, psychometric testing, performance appraisal, or formal or informal feedback, then use this. If there has been none,

Strengths	What are you good at, both generally in your job and your social skills and, specifically, as a manager and leader? How do you know? Would others agree with your assessment?
Weaknesses	What are the aspects of your job, your social skills or your performance as a manager and leader that are below the standard you believe is needed? How do you know? Would others agree with your assessment?
Opportunities	Are there opportunities for you to get training or use flexible learning materials or e-learning, be coached or mentored, use work shadowing or work experience, belong to networks or do research? How accessible are these? Who are the gatekeepers (who controls access) for any of these opportunities? How well do you take advantage of them?
Threats	Are any of these learning opportunities likely to be less easily available in the future? If you do not develop as a manager and leader, are you likely to suffer any disadvantages?

Figure 5.3   SWOT analysis

then look for opportunities to be assessed and invite feedback from those you lead and from your line manager and other colleagues. Try speaking to your organization's training and development people about the resources they have available to help you.

If they cannot help (or your organization does not have such a facility), there are books with assessment tools available; there are also plenty of tests available, both free and charged for, on the Internet – simply search on the terms 'leadership assessment' or 'psychometric tests' to find an enormous range. Choose with caution, looking carefully at the test provider to see if it appears legitimate, and be careful not to give out personal (or financial) details unless you are confident of the organization. Some of the free tests can be completed by others, assessing you, and you can compare their perceptions with yours.

Key idea

360° feedback

As you will know from your geometry at school, there are 360 degrees in a circle, and 360° feedback is simply about getting feedback from all around you, from those you lead, those you report to and those you work alongside. There are various IT-based tools used to collect 360° feedback, to ensure that people giving feedback can do so anonymously. If you have access to such tools then use them. If not, ask people to supply feedback, either face to face or by using some sort of assessment tool (there is one below) that you can ask people to fill in anonymously. Remember to stick to the advice about feedback given earlier and accept what people say as their perception of the truth, no matter how much you agree or disagree with it.

Leadership skills assessment

Figure 5.4 is a simple assessment of some of the skills that have been identified as important by research into leadership. It is based, in part, on the findings of a research project by Lew Perren (*Comparing Entrepreneurship and Leadership: A textual analysis*) on behalf of the Council for Excellence in Management and Leadership, in 2003. You can use this for self-assessment and also as a tool for structuring feedback from others. The outcomes of the exercise can then help you to decide your personal strengths and weaknesses.

Where do you want to be?

The outcomes of a personal SWOT, supported by various forms of assessment, can help you decide where you are. But where do you want to be? Leaders have to be able to provide a sense of direction and if they have no direction for themselves they will struggle to supply it to others. You need to be able to identify some vision for yourself, some idea of what it is you want to achieve personally and in your job. Think about what you want to achieve in your life, both in the immediate future and in the longer term.

These goals can cover:

- Your private and personal life (family, sport or recreation, hobbies or interests, physical ability or health)
- Your community or social role (involvement in religious, social, charitable or other activities)
- Your technical ability (i.e. not managerial or leadership, but functional responsibilities)
- Your career development (what kind of role or responsibility would you like to aim for, or would you like to make a complete career change?)
- Your management knowledge, skills and responsibilities
- Your leadership knowledge, skills and responsibilities.

Instructions for use

This is an assessment tool that can be used for self-assessment or by others as part of a feedback exercise. The 20 dimensions are not necessarily all that a leader needs, nor are they listed in any particular order of priority. You should assess yourself or the leader being assessed on each skill against the five levels:

5 Excellent – used by others as a model of best practice
4 Perfectly adequate – but could still make some improvements
3 Adequate – needs to improve, but not too bad
2 Not good – quite a lot of improvement needed
1 Very poor – needs to make wholesale improvement

The basis for your judgement would be the standard that you would expect from someone at that level in any well-run organization. This is a very personal judgement; do not allow your judgement to be clouded by what you would like to be true or feel that the leader would like to be told.

The scores are not meant to be added up, although they do have a maximum of 100. A total score of 50 could mean that someone ranks around 2 or 3 on all skills, or on 5 for about half of them and 1 on the others. It is the individual skills that matter, not the totals.

Leadership skills	Excellent – used by others as a model of best practice	Perfectly adequate – but could still make a few minor improvements	Adequate – needs to make some improvements but not too bad	Not good – quite a lot of improvement needed	Very poor – needs to make whole-sale improvement
a. Communicating information to other people	5	4	3	2	1
b. Listening and absorbing information from others	5	4	3	2	1
c. Demonstrating a sense of vision, a direction for self and others	5	4	3	2	1
d. Motivated to achieve personal goals, having personal drive	5	4	3	2	1
e. Dependable conscientious and persistent – gets things done	5	4	3	2	1
f. Able to motivate other people to work towards goals	5	4	3	2	1
g. Innovative, keen to try new ideas	5	4	3	2	1
h. Honest, shows integrity	5	4	3	2	1
i. Fair, treats people equitably	5	4	3	2	1
j. Trusted and trustworthy	5	4	3	2	1
k. Self-confident, willing to accept challenges	5	4	3	2	1
l. Able to assess and take appropriate risks	5	4	3	2	1
m. Emotionally stable but not afraid to show emotions, when appropriate	5	4	3	2	1
n. Sensitive to others' emotional state, caring about others	5	4	3	2	1
o. Willing to learn, not afraid to ask when meeting something new	5	4	3	2	1
p. Interested in and valuing others	5	4	3	2	1
q. Willing to make decisions and take responsibility	5	4	3	2	1
r. Working well in a team	5	4	3	2	1
s. Recognizing others' achievements	5	4	3	2	1
t. Technically competent	5	4	3	2	1

Figure 5.4 Leadership self-assessment

You do not have to share these with anyone, but discussing them with a line manager or training and development manager can help in alerting you to possibilities that you may not have considered and also in setting priorities for your goals. Think about setting long-, medium- and short-term goals for each area. Long-term can be five or ten years or more in the future; medium-term can be two to five years ahead; and short-term within the next few months to two years. Use timescales that seem relevant to you at your age and your stage of life.

Now set some priorities for your goals, using the following scale:

1 This is absolutely critical – I must do this for my own sense of self-worth.

2 This is important to me and I would be disappointed not to achieve it.

3 This is quite important and it would be good to achieve it.

4 This would be nice to achieve, but is not that important.

Deciding on these priorities tests a leader's commitment and motivation, personal honesty and integrity. Saying that something is a first priority – that it is absolutely critical ('I must do this for my own sense of self-worth') – means that its achievement takes precedence over all other possible development goals. Before saying that something is 'priority one', you need to ask yourself how much time, effort and resource you are prepared to devote to its achievement. If you are not prepared to devote much of your own time, put much effort in, or spend any of your own resources, then how critical is it to you, personally, as opposed to, say, your employer or line manager?

Setting priorities is not the same as determining how soon a goal should be achieved. The distinction between urgent and important is just as relevant here. Some low priority goals may be urgent, as the opportunity to acquire or use them may be available soon, and may not recur for some time. On the other hand, if they are not acquired or used, it would be no great loss. Priority is primarily about importance; urgency is about when the goal needs to be achieved.

How do you get there?

In Chapter 4, talking about planning, we suggested that a leader focuses on the direction of travel at least as much as on the destination. This is as true of personal development goals as it is of any other type of goal. Personal development as a leader is a direction not a destination, because you can never stop improving. The goals you set for yourself are there to help you keep to the direction you are travelling in. The way you travel must take account of the opportunities and threats you identified in your personal SWOT. It includes the range of techniques mentioned earlier, such as:

- Formal courses, including longer ones leading to qualifications in leadership and management, and to shorter ones that develop specific knowledge and skills
- Research and reading, to develop knowledge and understanding of specific tasks or topics
- Coaching and mentoring in the workplace, to develop knowledge, apply skills and reflect on them
- Work shadowing or work experience, to observe others or experience roles, to develop knowledge and practice skills
- Action learning sets, experimentation and workplace application of knowledge and skills, to develop knowledge, apply skills and reflect on them.

A learning style preference may well make some of these options appear more attractive than others. However, the best learning comes from a mix of activities that will support working round the whole experiential learning cycle.

Detailed planning should only be for the short to medium term, as circumstances change and the effectiveness of particular strategies needs to be reviewed periodically, asking 'How well is this helping me achieve my goals?' Never forget, the plan is the route map not the purpose of the journey.

Reflection

1 Following the steps outlined here, carry out your own personal SWOT to determine where you are now, using existing performance appraisals, and assessments, as well as any other assessment tools you can identify as being useful.

2 Decide on your short-, medium- and longer-term goals, in discussion with those whose opinion and help you value (e.g. training personnel, your line manager, colleagues and members of your family).

3 Prepare a plan for the next six months to a year to develop yourself as a more effective leader, focusing on the knowledge and skills that you have identified as being priorities, but also recognize the urgency for developing them and the opportunities available to do so.

Summary

- Leadership combines a range of cognitive, affective and psycho-motor skills, and leaders need to accept personal responsibility for developing these skills.

- The most effective learning occurs when people move through a cycle of concrete experience which, through observation and critical reflection, they make sense of, leading to abstract conceptualization and generalization (identifying underpinning principles and patterns) allowing them to plan active experimentation to test out new ideas and try out other ways of acting.

- People appear to favour certain parts of this learning cycle and, possibly, learning through particular senses (seeing, hearing or doing). It can help leaders to be aware of these preferences in order to ensure that they complete the cycle, to work through all four stages and to appreciate its full implications.

- Learning is not a solitary activity; the best learning occurs with the support of others, through approaches such as action learning sets and networking. Leaders who take responsibility for their own learning should not think that this means that they have to do it alone – in fact, the best leaders always look to others to help them as much as possible.

- Making the most of opportunities to develop yourself also means having a clear direction and purpose to your learning and this, in turn, means being prepared to assess your starting point (Where are you now?), your goal (Where do you want to be?) and the best route between these two points (How do you get there?).

Notes

1 For example *Introducing Leadership* or its sister publication, *Introducing Management*, by Kate Williams, also published by Butterworth-Heinemann.

2 Such as *Super Series*, the management development programme published by Pergamon Flexible Learning.
3 NLP was originally developed by John Grinder, a Professor at University of California and Richard Bandler, a student there. It is a combination of aspects of neuroscience, psychotherapy and linguistics, and its techniques are used by coaches, counsellors and trainers. Many academics are critical of it, but many practitioners find its tools and techniques useful in their work.

6 Organizations, structures and roles

Leaders do not work in isolation; they need people to lead (their followers) and they usually work within some sort of formal structure (the organization). This chapter is about organizations, what they are for, how they are structured and what people do within them, their role. To make sense of this we will also look at important issues for leaders such as relationships, power, responsibility and accountability, and introduce the idea of *systems* as a way of making sense of how organizations work as they do. In the process, we will see how the leadership role and performance of first line and middle managers is shaped by these issues.

What are organizations for?

We have all seen the images on TV of a crowd protesting angrily, faced by police officers in riot gear with plastic shields and batons ready. We immediately recognize which group is which.

Both groups are operating as organized bodies, but in different ways. The crowd is organized around a more or less common sense of purpose and this shared purpose gives the crowd a rationale for existing and an ability to act collectively, responding to what individuals do. If one person does something that others support, they will copy that behaviour and, if a sufficient number take it up, this can cause the whole crowd to act as if they are coordinated. Such a crowd is self-organizing when individual goals and the willingness to act on them coincide. However, some people will be more influential than others and can take leadership of such a crowd by persuading enough people that they can help them towards their goal.

Surprisingly, far fewer police officers can prevent the crowd from succeeding by using their superior organizational ability (as well as superior force, but the best rely mainly on organization). They, too, have a clear purpose, but this is accompanied by a plan of

99

operation, effective control and coordination of the resources available, and skilled people and appropriate resources. As a result they do not need to rely on chance for their efforts to be organized and directed towards their goal. Despite this superior organization, the crowd can sometimes succeed if their level of commitment to their goal is sufficiently strong to over-ride their natural desire for safety. It is not their greater size that can give them the edge on its own, but this level of commitment to their goal that does it, imposing sufficient organization on their disorder to overcome the managed order and strategy of the police.

What has this got to do with the way that most organizations operate? Because management (in the way that it is usually defined, as planning, organization, command, coordinate and control) is needed to ensure that resources are used effectively, but leadership, by harnessing the drive and commitment of people, can often achieve as much without the formal structures, hierarchies and clearly defined roles that are commonly thought to be necessary. But the ideal way of working is to harness the strength of formal structures, roles and relationships to the goal-directed and committed behaviour of informal organization. This is why, throughout *Introducing Leadership*, we continue to argue that leadership and management are not alternatives. Successful organizations combine both to achieve their goals as efficiently and effectively as possible.

Organizational purpose

All organizations exist for a purpose, although at times it is not always easy to see what that purpose is! The purpose may be defined at two levels:

1   The general, higher level purpose that distinguishes:

   - private sector organizations, whose primary purpose is to make a profit
   - public sector organizations, which usually exist to create a healthy (e.g. hospitals), educated (e.g. colleges) and safe (e.g. police) society, and
   - voluntary (or 'third') sector organizations, which are usually concerned with improving the general welfare of society, animals or the physical environment in some way.

2   The specific purpose that defines what any particular organization actually does to make a profit; to create a healthy, educated

and safe society; or to improve the welfare of society, animals or the physical environment.

For example, any private sector organization would say that it aims to make a profit in order to provide its owners (investors) with a sufficient return on their investment to reward them for making the money available and for the risk they have taken. However, this is not a purpose that will inspire its employees to use their abilities to the full. To do this, it needs a more specific purpose, associated with the industry it is in and the market it serves, that provides owners, employees, customers and suppliers with a shared understanding of what it is for. This is a challenge that all private sector organizations face. Making increased profitability their sole purpose may please investors, but offers nothing to the people working hard everyday to achieve it. That is one reason that some companies offer profit-related bonuses and share options (the opportunity to buy shares at below market price), to provide employees with a reason to achieve profit targets.

Purpose in the private sector: small and medium sized enterprises

The vast majority (99.8 per cent) of private sector organizations are small and medium sized enterprises (SMEs), ranging from sole traders (individuals working on their own or with a few employees) to companies with as many as 250 employees. Despite their number they account for just over half the workforce, because of their relatively small size. However, this size means that they rarely have to spell out their purpose in detail, for the simple reason that their leaders and managers can make it clear to the whole workforce fairly easily, through their words and their deeds. In many of these organizations, especially the smallest, these leaders and managers are also the owners of the business, which gives them even greater force in demonstrating what they care about.

Owners and leaders who are crazy about quality or customer service, or about clean and tidy workplaces, good time-keeping or hard work, set a clear purpose for the organization without having to say: 'This is our mission ...'. Equally, those who are sloppy, lazy, uncaring and rude to customers can have just as powerful an effect on the business. This personal commitment is something we return to, below.

Purpose in the private sector: larger companies

It is all too easy to divide private sector business into two groups, SMEs and 'big business' as if all large firms are the same. The reality is that a firm with several hundred employees, all working on one site, has more in common with a medium sized business than with a massive multinational operating across five continents. However, larger businesses do tend to have more problems in making their purpose clear, because the people who lead the business are much further away from the people they lead, sometimes many thousands of miles further away! This is why such businesses are more likely to express their purpose through *mission* or *vision statements*. These spell out what the organization is aiming to do and to be. In Chapter 4 we said that:

Whereas the manager focuses on objectives and targets, the leader is concerned with mission *and* values.

- *A mission statement is a way of setting direction, to say what you (your organization, department or team) want to be, whom you want to serve and what drives you.*
- *A values statement spells out the drivers and the beliefs under-pinning them in more detail.*

This is because mission and values statements provide the direction that is an essential feature of leadership. The larger the organization, the greater the need for this direction to be made explicit, so that everyone is clear where they are heading, and why.

Purpose in public sector organizations

A clear purpose is just as important for public sector organizations as it is for the private sector. In fact, it is possibly more important, because there is no over-riding profit motive to guide decision-making. This lack of a profit motive does not mean that a public sector organization lacks purpose, but that the purpose does need to be made explicit. Although a public sector organization (like a government department, local school or hospital) ought to make the best use of the money available, it needs a better sense of 'why' it exists. Just like private sector organizations, size is important. A small primary school will be much like a small business, with a leader and manager (head teacher) easily visible, spending most of the time teaching like other staff, and setting the working style of the organization.

On the other hand, the head of a large Government agency (like the Benefits Agency or HM Revenue and Customs) will never meet all the staff employed in the organization. That is why these larger organizations need to have a clear statement of purpose at least as much as private sector organizations, and probably more so. Without one, it becomes too easy for such organizations to exist for the benefit of their employees, with the quality of services and the efficiency with which resources are used taking second place to individuals' own needs. This is not their fault, but poor leadership. Just as the crowd in the city square is often just a disorganized mob without leadership, an organization without a clear purpose must lack leadership, with the result that people follow their own personal goals.

Purpose in voluntary (or third) sector organizations

These types of organizations differ quite markedly from both the public and private sectors because they can often be defined purely in terms of their purpose – to relieve poverty, to protect children, to preserve wildlife, etc. However, they are probably more diverse in their range of purposes than any private or public sector organizations. The small charity helping the child victims of the nuclear catastrophe in Chernobyl is in this category of organizations, alongside building societies and trades unions ('mutual societies' that support their members to buy houses and obtain protection at work, respectively), as are the Red Cross, Cancer Research UK and Oxfam. However, this diversity does not stop these organizations from having clarity of purpose. In fact, their diversity stems from being organizations that have been developed to serve very specific purposes.

Does the fact that organizations in the different sectors tend to have different purposes mean that these purposes will be quite distinctive? Do the different sectors operate so differently that you could tell them apart just by looking at their mission statements or statements of aims? See what you think – Figure 6.1 has three mission statements: one is from a private sector organization; one from a public sector organization; and one from a voluntary or third sector organization. Can you tell which is which?

All three organizations are involved in education and training, in its broadest sense. One is a major multinational, one a Government department and the third is a membership organization and the UK's

1 'To be the indispensable information provider for our target customers in selected professional markets.'

2 'To provide distinctive, innovative and comprehensive services to support all individuals and organizations wishing to initiate, improve and maintain their capability in leadership and management.'

3 'Creating opportunity, releasing potential and achieving excellence for all.'

Figure 6.1 Three mission statements

largest provider of qualifications in its particular specialist area. Have you decided which is which now? The first statement is the corporate goal of Reed Elsevier plc, which is quoted on the Dutch and UK stock exchanges and which owns Butterworth-Heinemann, publishers of this book. The second is the mission statement of the Institute of Leadership and Management, a registered charity owned by and working for the benefit of its members, the people studying for its qualifications and the organizations which run courses for them. The third is what the Department for Education and Skills describes as the purpose for which it was established.

What has this to do with leadership? As we saw in Chapter 1, leadership is all about setting direction, and an organization without direction is leaderless. Having a set of aims or a mission statement does not mean that an organization is being led, but without any clear sense of purpose, a reason for existing, leadership is impossible. Such a purpose does not need to be spelled out – as we have seen, in many smaller organizations the purpose is well understood without ever being written down. Equally, what is said may bear little resemblance to what the organization is actually about. All too often, such statements are carefully crafted, ready to be included in annual reports and obscure parts of the corporate website, and ignored by everyone the rest of the time. One of the key tasks of leaders at all levels is to make sure that the organization's day-to-day activities work to fulfil its purpose. However, this is only possible if all leaders are working together, whether it is the chief executive or an operational team leader.

Reflection

- Does your organization have a mission statement or statement of aims?
- Is it well known?

- Is it useful in giving you (and those you lead) a sense of direction?
- How well do the organization's leaders actively promote this purpose, by their words and their actions?
- What conclusions does this lead you to about how well the organization is being led?

Personal commitment

Coming back to the angry crowd in the town square, if they have a purpose that they are all sufficiently committed to, they can do amazing things. In Ukraine, in 2004's 'Orange Revolution', enough people were sufficiently committed to protest against electoral fraud and intimidation that they compelled the courts to order that the elections be re-run, leading to internationally recognized free and fair elections. The police and army, although controlled by the Government, lacked the same level of commitment. Purpose, on its own, is not enough. People have to feel that they want to make the purpose real and, while organizations can have *purpose*, only people can have *commitment*. The role of leaders is to build that commitment. Managers can organize resources, design systems, monitor activities and outcomes, but it is the role of leaders to build commitment to achieve the goals that the organization exists for.

What is 'commitment'? Commitment is the extent to which a person feels a sense of emotional involvement with the idea of achieving a goal. It is what makes an athlete go out training on a cold and wet morning; it is what makes parents give up their own pleasures and time to enable their children to do what they want to do. The emotional involvement is the desire to do something that may offer little chance of success or a very long-term and vague payback for the investment, but getting satisfaction from having done what one believes is the *right thing* to do. You will remember from Chapter 2 that the 'right thing' is a moral judgement, based on a person's own set of values and beliefs, and commitment is only possible if the actions needed are in line with these values and beliefs.

This is important in making sense of effective leadership, because if leaders set out in a direction which they believe is morally right – if they believe in what is being aimed for – then they will have a personal commitment. This does not mean that they have to be very high-minded (although some organizations do have aims that involve saving lives or the very planet we live on), but they must be sufficient to make someone feel that they are worthwhile. If you look back at the three purpose statements on page 104, you can judge how well they encourage a sense of moral worth, that someone might feel it is worth making a commitment to.

Some voluntary sector organizations, such as those working to relieve poverty and destitution, can easily get that commitment from all their staff, many of whom work for them precisely because their personal values are in line with the organization's aims, often doing so as volunteers or on below average pay. This does not mean that they need less leadership or management, because that commitment can be just as problematic as having none at all. Whereas people in organizations with no clear purpose can behave as if all that matters is following the rules and procedures irrespective of whether or not it is being effective, highly committed people can treat rules and procedures as, at best, guidelines as to what should be done and, at worst, as obstacles in their path, to be overcome! Their commitment needs to be channelled into achieving the organizational purpose, or it can easily produce a lot of very busy fools, running around fast and achieving nothing.

For a private sector organization, gaining such commitment can be hard but is achievable if it makes a link between the things that motivate the people it employs and its purpose. People normally want to do a good job and would far rather work for an organization that wants to produce good quality goods or services, offering excellent value for money, one that treats its employees with respect, offering appropriate rates of pay for work in good conditions, and that operates in ways that are safe and do not harm the environment. As a leader in such an organization, your role is very much to demonstrate that these goals are real, and to ensure that the people you lead recognize how easy it is for them to make a commitment to the organization and support these principles.

Conversely, an organization that tries to milk customers (or service users) by providing sub-standard goods or services that represent poor value for money, treats its employees with contempt, pays them badly, makes them work in unsafe or unhealthy conditions, engenders no commitment and finds that it gets little support and even less hard work from people. Effective leadership in such an organization is almost impossible; all that managers are likely to be doing is trying to control people, to prevent them from doing more harm than the organization is doing to itself!

Organization structures

Medieval society was rigidly structured, with the monarch at the top, supported by layers of nobility (itself with several ranks), down to the serfs at the bottom. This hierarchical system with its ranks and its centralized power looks, well, medieval. Yet many organizations are structured in much the same way today. The Chief Executive or Chairman (or, very occasionally, Chairwoman) sits at the top of a pyramid of power, with individuals only allowed to make limited decisions affecting their immediate area. What is more, the pyramid is often divided up into self-contained units (like medieval baronies), each of which is then further subdivided, with communication, accountability and control all happening vertically, up the long chain of command and control that leads to the apex where real power lies.

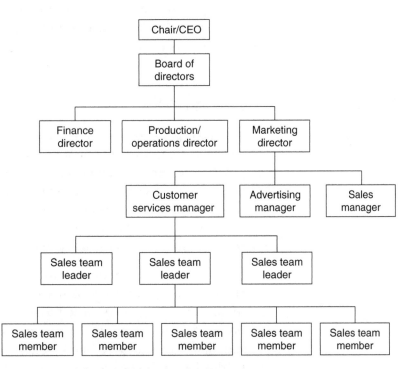

Figure 6.2   A hierarchical organization

This hierarchical structure is still common, even if attempts have been made to reduce some of the different levels and the barriers that tend to exist between divisions. These changes have to be made because:

- Too many layers of control prevent fast and informed decision-making, as problems get referred up to the people allowed to make them who may be too far removed from the reality of the situation to make properly informed decisions. In the worst cases, nobody is prepared or allowed to make decisions and everything, no matter how small or unimportant, gets referred up to the top (a common problem in smaller organizations, especially as they expand and grow larger).

- Problems get considered in isolation from the rest of the organization, and the consequences of decisions for others are not considered. In the worst cases, different divisions become competitive, regarding winning over other divisions as more important than working towards achieving the organization's goals.

All too often the managers of such organizations are limited in their behaviour by their perception of power as *zero sum*, and this prevents them being effective leaders. Power gets hoarded by those at the top of the hierarchy and those lower down are limited in their ability to make decisions and respond effectively to customers, suppliers or co-workers.

Key idea

Zero sum

The perception of power as *zero sum* means that people believe there is a given amount of power, and that by giving power to others you diminish the amount you have left for yourself, because there is a finite amount. The alternative way of thinking is to see power as *non-zero sum*, where sharing power with others does not diminish the power you possess, but increases the total amount of power.

The zero sum assumption treats organizational power like electric power; plug a 500 W machine into a 1000 W generator and there is only 500 W left to use. This seems logical and obeys the laws of physics. However, seeing power as non-zero sum treats it more like kindness; if you treat someone kindly that often encourages them to treat others kindly. Two people being kind to others does not decrease the amount of kindness elsewhere, it increases the stock of kindness in the world. This is because kindness – like organizational power – does not have physical mass, nor is it created from mass, unlike electric power. We cannot create energy from nothing but we can create kindness from nothing, and we can create organizational power from nothing. Effective leaders understand this and know that by delegating responsibility for decision-making they do not lose power but add to the total amount of power in the organization.

From function to process

The conventional, hierarchical structure (like the example in Figure 6.2) is generally organized around *functions*. A function is a set of specialist activities that share the same set of knowledge and skills, equipment and other resources. Common examples of functional areas include:

- Warehousing and stock control (in a factory)
- Radiography (in a hospital)
- Loss adjusters (in an insurance company)
- Customer service centre or accounts department (in any organization).

This type of structure allows organizations to achieve greater control over how resources are used, enabling them to be combined together in ways that ensure maximum efficiency in their use, and create coherent career structures for specialist staff. However, what works well for the organization may not work well for the customer, client or service user. For them, the different functions can be a series of hurdles to be overcome (Figure 6.3).

Figure 6.3   The customer's perspective

This is the process as experienced by the customer (or service user), one that can often involve long waits between stages and exceptionally poor communications, as messages have to be passed on from one person to another. A process that is organized around the process rather than the function would mean having a multi-functional team dealing direct with the customer (Figure 6.4).

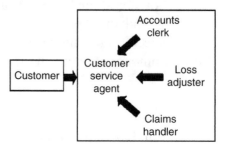

Figure 6.4 An integrated focus

The multi-functional team involves people of different backgrounds with different expertise, working together to complete interrelated tasks. For customers, this means that the service can be completed more quickly and more effectively, raising their perceptions of the organization and adding value to the service provided. For the people in the team this can mean feeling that this has been a job well done (*job satisfaction*), more variety (*job enlargement* – the chance to get involved in different aspects of the job), and a greater sense of being in control of their own workload (*empowerment*). Organizations have often created *cells* or *zones* in their workspaces so that teams are physically located together, separate from other teams, to enable them to communicate easily and to identify clearly with their team and their customers.

The change from a functional to process organization became very popular in the 1990s under the banner of Business Process Re-engineering (BPR), particularly after the publication of a book by Michael Hammer and James Champney called *Re-engineering the Corporation: A manifesto for business revolution* (Nicholas Brealey: 1995). Unfortunately, it also became associated with de-layering (reducing the number of management layers) and large-scale redundancies of middle managers. This had two effects:

1 It got re-engineering (and its associated techniques, such as team-working) a bad name, as it was seen as being primarily about cost-cutting rather than improving processes

2 It meant many organizations lost knowledge, as the middle managers who left often knew best how the processes worked.

The mistake many senior managers made was failing to recognize that the revolution that was needed was not just in the structure of their organizations, but in their own thinking. A functional structure is based on simple processes in a complex organization (each person or group is specialized, making processes simple, but it takes a lot of these specialist processes to complete the whole process), whereas a process-focused structure is a simple organization with complex processes. It is simple because it consists of multiple teams operating independently, so work does not have to move across internal boundaries, but each team undertakes complex processes, drawing on many different functional specialisms.

This new structure looks simple but is very difficult to control, because responsibility for processes lies with teams and their leaders. In particular, it can mean that different teams work out different ways to deal with the same problems. Also, since senior managers may themselves be specialists, it can mean that they no longer head up their specialism in the organization, at least as a line manager. They may have to move into more of an 'internal consultancy' role. The challenge for such senior managers is to switch their emphasis from how a job is done to what is being produced, from the process to the outcomes. (There is more about BPR in Chapter 13.)

Multi-functional teams are not necessarily the only way of creating a focus on the customer or service user; alternative ways of organizing people with similar goals include:

- *Matrix structures*, where a conventional functional structure, organized vertically (as in Figure 6.2), is balanced by a horizontal structure based on customer types or characteristics, balancing the focus on the technical expertise of the functional structure with an equal focus on the specific needs of customers or markets. Leadership in matrix structures can be challenging, because there may well be conflicts along the two dimensions, and those controlling resources (usually on the functional or vertical arm) often have more power than others. Leadership in this situation requires particularly effective negotiation skills and the ability to build consensus between people with different goals.

- *Project team structures*, which are common in organizations that primarily undertake unique tasks with a specific start and end date, such as civil engineering or IT and communications systems. In effect, individuals have no fixed position in a structure, as they move between different temporary or fixed term multi-functional teams. They can be a member of different teams at the same time, and be leader of one team and an ordinary member of another. Leadership in project teams requires strong communication and coordination skills, because team members may be dispersed around an organization, and even around the world. It also means being good at building teams quickly and helping the team to break up painlessly.

A systems view of organizations

The switch of emphasis demanded by Business Process Re-engineering, from 'how' to 'what', from functions to processes, means being able to see the organization as a system. A system is any organized set of elements that combine together to produce an outcome, of any sort. A car engine is a system, the components combining to produce automotive power. A tree is a system, combining nutrients from the soil with energy from the sun to produce wood and leaf. The whole world is a system, taking in energy from the sun to enable life. All systems can be pictured in a simple diagram as shown in Figure 6.5.

Figure 6.5   A basic system model

Organizations are special types of systems, often called socio-technical systems, because they are made up of people and the equipment and other resources they use. One of the features of people is that they think, have personalities and emotions, and follow rules only if they think they should do, or are made to. Systems like car engines or trees do not think, or have personalities and emotions, nor do they disobey the rules of physics, engineering or biology.

One writer and academic, Peter Checkland[1], puts great emphasis on the importance of the *world-view* (a translation of the German word *Weltanschaung*) of:

- the *actors* (people working in the system) and
- the *owners* (the people responsible for the system – shareholders, board members, etc.)

in shaping how the system works. This world-view is the set of experiences, beliefs and values that affect the way that individuals perceive reality and how they respond to that perception.

In other words, an organization is not like a machine that can be assembled from parts that can be replaced easily and expect the same results. The more responsibility that people in teams are given for their own tasks, the more they cause the system to change. They also tend to erect *boundaries* around themselves, defining what is inside their system (what they are responsible for, what rules apply, etc.) and what is outside it. This can be positive, because it means that the team accepts responsibility, but it can also be negative, because it can cause the team to exclude other people's ideas and practices. These are all issues that we shall look at in more detail in the next chapter.

Organizational roles

Roles are the part that people play in organizations. Peter Checkland labelled the people in systems as 'actors' and roles are the parts that actors play. It is useful to recognize that we all play several roles in our lives. We can be a manager at work, a parent and a husband or wife at home, a school governor, secretary of a community group and a student at an Adult Education art class. Which of these roles is truly 'us'? None of them and all of them. We take on the appropriate characteristics of the role when we adopt it, and can shift from one to another. Problems occur when we meet the same people in two different roles – because roles give us:

- rules of behaviour (how we should behave towards each other)

- authority over others, and others' authority over us

- a sense of 'self' (of who we are).

When we meet people outside the normal setting we are unsure as to which role to play. The more comfortable we are in all our roles, the less of a problem we find switching roles – we do not allow each role to take over and act like someone we are not. Instead, we make each of the roles our own and stamp our own personality on them. Let us look at each of these three characteristics of roles, in turn, and see how this works.

Rules of behaviour

All societies have rules about behaviour, which is why we often find going abroad difficult. Ignoring issues like language, just ordering a drink in a café can be highly problematic. It is the same in organizations, they have written and unwritten rules that shape what is done and what is not done. Written rules will be in the organization's policies and procedures, and in job descriptions, but the unwritten rules are more extensive and subtle. They are part of the *culture* of the organization, what has been described as 'the way we do things around here'.

Key idea

The Hawthorne studies

One of the earliest, and most famous, studies exploring how organizations work was done at the Hawthorne works of the General Electric company in the USA in the 1930s. The objective was to explore how changes to the way that work was done would affect productivity. These experiments identified two significant effects:

- Groups of workers tended to establish *norms*, work rates that were sustainable for the full working day, enforced by subtle social pressures on those working too hard (showing up the others) or not hard enough (and obviously slacking)

- The attention paid to workers tended to improve performance, irrespective of what the experimenters were doing, something now known as the *Hawthorne Effect*, because it can distort social experiments by changing behaviour simply through studying it.

Cultural norms, the social rules that govern behaviour, are very powerful and vary from country to country, organization to organization and even from team to team. Effective leaders understand the importance of rules of behaviour and recognize when conflicts occur between different sets of rules, especially between the official rules that the organization has set and the unofficial rules that are enforced by co-workers. Wherever possible, such rules need to be harnessed and used to achieve the goals of the organization, but there are times when such rules are counter-productive or even dangerous. For example, a culture that encourages unsafe risk-taking or discourages safe practice cannot be tolerated. As a member of the team (one role) you may be tempted to abide by the team's rules, but as a manager and the leader of the team (another role), you also have to make sure that the organization's rules are observed, so far as possible. You may judge that some rules are less important than others, but you should have good reasons, in line with the organization's goals and values, if you choose to break them. Leadership involves taking difficult and sometimes unpopular decisions and sticking to them consistently. Where the official or unofficial rules of behaviour need changing they should be changed – there is more about how to do this in Chapter 13.

Authority

The second important element of a leadership role is authority, authority over others and others' authority over us. Authority combines two sub-elements, *power* (which we have already mentioned) and *accountability*. Formal power comes to leaders from those with more power and they are, in turn, accountable for how they use that power. Roles in an organization are often defined in terms of the formal power that people have who occupy those roles. There can be varying degrees of power according to how much has been delegated to a role, such as:

- the level of input someone has into a decision to hire or fire
- what size of purchase the role holder can authorize
- how much change to processes, roles systems, structures and other people's roles that the people in particular roles are allowed to make.

This kind of formal organizational power is balanced by accountability for how that power is exercised. Accountability in a role means that the person occupying the role must show that the power was wielded appropriately and wisely – *appropriate* meaning that the power was used in the way that was expected and not abused or misused, and *wise* in making the right decisions (at least most of the time).

Wisdom in decision-making is the hardest part of any leadership role, since it combines both meanings of 'right' – making decisions that are in line with the rules and procedures to produce the desired outcomes (doing things right), and making decisions that are right, morally. Effective leaders are aware of both meanings of right and make sure that they do what is required by the organization and what is morally right. What is more, if there is ever a conflict between these two ('doing things right' and 'doing the right thing'), leaders will always strive to do the right thing, accepting the responsibility that comes with being accountable in their role.

As we have seen, power is non-zero sum, so it is possible for leaders to delegate power to those they lead without losing any power themselves, so long as the organization allows delegation. However, accountability cannot be delegated alongside delegated power; leaders are accountable for the decisions made in their name, whether or not they have made the decisions themselves. This is as true for the power that is delegated to you as it is for the power you may delegate to others. Ultimately, all leaders, at any level, are accountable for the decisions made by those they have delegated power to. When making decisions you should always respect the trust put in you by those you are accountable to as they, in turn, are accountable to others for what they have delegated to you.

The formal power that comes with a particular role has been described as *position power*, because it arises from the position one holds – it means that you are able to tell someone to do something and expect that they will do it. However, effective leaders are also able to call on their *personal power* in getting things done. Personal power is independent of position or role, and means that people will do what you want them to do because of the respect and trust they hold for you as a person, not because of the role you occupy. Position power is tied to the role; personal power is tied to the person. To develop personal power you must be seen to be worthy of it, since it is delegated up from those you lead, in the same way that positional power is delegated down by people in authority over you. What is more, you are just as accountable for your personal power to those who have granted it to you as you are to those who delegated your position power.

Reflection

Who do you know who has 'personal power', the informal authority to make decisions or give advice that is granted to him or her over and above any power that comes with the formal role held? What are the qualities or behaviours that has earned this person the personal power?

In Chapter 4 we described the principal characteristics of leaders as:

- Acting honestly, with integrity, equity and fairness
- Having insights into your own personality, attitudes, motivation and emotions
- Communicating well with others
- Setting a clear direction and a good example to others.

It is through these or similar characteristics that personal power is derived because it is through them that you build up the respect and trust that leaders need to make people want to follow them, not just to follow them because they have no choice to do otherwise – the kind of followership that people wielding positional power rely on. The difference between the two is that positional power is only useable when in that role, and it can only demand that people abide by the official rules. Positional power cannot get people to put in that little bit extra, to get things done that would not otherwise be possible.

A sense of 'self'

The third aspect of the different roles we play is that they define who we are. The person who is a manager at work, a parent and a husband or wife at home, a school governor, secretary of a community group and a student at an Adult Education art class, will introduce themselves to others in a different way according to the circumstances. At the school gate we might be a parent and a school governor; at a party we are so-and-so's wife or husband or partner; at the Adult Education Centre we are an art student. One of the first things we do when we meet people for the first time is to learn what role they play, and usually this means their role at work. This is why people who are unemployed often lack self-esteem – they are unable to describe themselves in the terms that other people use (I'm a customer services team leader or a production supervisor).

Effective leaders occupy different roles as well; the difference is that they are good at using their experiences in different roles to improve their performance as leaders. They will learn from being a parent that it is easier to get children to do what you want them to do if you provide them with a reason for doing so that reflects their own motivation rather than by saying 'because I tell you to' (using your position power). As a school governor, a leader has to learn to work in a consensual way with other governors, all of whom are volunteers, and with a professional head teacher who will often have more knowledge but not always more wisdom. As a student, a leader learns to respect those with more knowledge and experience and to learn from them.

Playing more than one role, being aware of the demands of these different roles, being able to respond to them and allowing the experiences from one role to inform the others helps to develop us as individuals. Leaders are not one-dimensional figures who only do one thing. They should constantly seek new challenges and opportunities to develop their knowledge and experience to become fully rounded, to stretch themselves to learn what they are capable of achieving.

Key idea

The Johari Window

The Johari Window model was developed by American psychologists Joseph Luft and Harry Ingham in the 1950s, while researching group dynamics. It contains four elements or 'areas':

1 What we know about ourselves which is also known by others – the **open area**
2 What we do not know about ourselves but which others do know – **blind area**
3 What we know about ourselves but which others do not know – **hidden area**
4 What both we and others do not know about ourselves – **unknown area**

This grid illustrates these four aspects of ourselves; the challenge for us all is to maximize the size of the open area, to recognize our own strengths and weaknesses and to allow others to see them (to move them from our 'hidden area').

	Known by self	Unknown by self
Known by others	**Open area**	**Blind area**
Unknown by others	**Hidden area**	**Unknown area**

We should also attempt to move knowledge about ourselves from our 'blind area' by seeking and accepting feedback from others, and to reduce our unknown area by taking the opportunity to try new experiences and take on new challenges.

Leaders are not navel-gazers, always thinking and talking about themselves or obsessed about their own lives. However, they are self-aware and aware of how others are reacting to them, in all their different roles. This is a key part of learning and development, improving the skills and knowledge needed to be effective in the role.

Summary

- Different types of organization exist to serve different purposes, and leaders must recognize what those purposes are and be alert to their effect on the behaviour of those they lead, harnessing individuals' own motivation to achieve the organization's goals.

- Organizations exist for a purpose, and the structure of the organization should help people to work most effectively to secure that purpose. Conventional organizations were organized hierarchically (power and control coming down from the top) and people grouped functionally (by what they did) but, increasingly, organizations have attempted to reorganize into multi-functional teams around processes (what the customer or service user experiences), to become more responsive to their needs. This places more responsibility on team leaders for managing complex processes and requires more senior managers to delegate power and relinquish their own control.

- A key element of all organization structures is the roles that different people play within them. Roles exist to define rules of behaviour (how we should behave towards each other), what authority some people have over others and to give us a sense of 'self', of who we are as individuals.
  - Leaders need to recognize that both formal and informal rules exist, and that informal rules can often be more significant in shaping behaviour.

- They also need to be aware of their positional and personal power, how they are acquired and to whom they are accountable for using this power.
- Finally, they should reflect on the different roles they play, how this defines who they are and how they can learn from these different roles to develop and improve their leadership performance.

Note

1 Peter Checkland's 'soft systems methodology' is described more fully in his book *Systems Thinking, Systems Practice* (Wiley: 1998), in which he defines systems in terms of the *actors*, *owners* and their *world-views*, the *transformation* (what is being done), the *customers* (product/service users) and the *environment* (the external influences on the system).

7 Getting the best out of individuals

Everyone is different. Some differences are immediately obvious – man or woman, old or young, not to mention the vast range of physical differences reflecting ethnicity, family heritage and plain chance – but most significant are those differences stemming from personality, from different emotional sensitivity and from beliefs, values and attitudes. Some of these differences are primarily genetic, inherited from our parents; others are the results of our upbringing, our family, social, educational and economic background. Increasingly, it is becoming clear that neither operates independently of the other – we are the product of the interaction between our genes and upbringing.

What has this got to do with leadership? Simply, that effective leadership depends on a contract between leaders and their followers, in which each person is offered something personal and specific to their needs in return for their commitment to follow the leader. Whereas managers are primarily concerned with human resources, with the number and ability of employees, leaders are concerned with people as individuals, with specific needs and ambitions. Managers develop and implement performance management systems, incentives and disciplinary procedures. Leaders understand what makes individuals tick, how to get the best out of them and challenge them when they are not performing as well as they could.

As we have argued right the way through *Introducing Leadership*, this does not mean that leadership is somehow better than management, it is just different, and it serves a different purpose. Managers create the systems and procedures within which leaders work. Managers without leadership ability rely on these mechanisms to maximize the performance of the organization. Effective leaders use these as a framework within which to get the best out of each individual, treating everyone equally and fairly, but not necessarily the same.

This chapter is all about these individual differences, how to recognize them and how to use them to enable people to achieve what they are capable of and fulfil their potential. In Chapter 8 this theme is continued by looking at people in groups and teams, at the difference between the two, and how to get the best performance out of them both.

Individual differences

What do we mean by 'individual differences'? It is easy to think that when children are born they are like a blank sheet of paper on which is written their personality and emotions, in the same way that they learn to walk and talk. But walking and talking are partly hard-wired, which is why we can walk on our two hind legs and speak, while most other animals cannot. We learn to use both abilities, but the latent ability exists already (for nearly everyone), and the same is true for most other facets of our individuality.

- A tall couple will probably have tall children, but many children today are taller than their parents because of improved nutrition and housing.

- Musical parents often pass on their interest and ability to their children, but musical prodigies can appear in families without any great interest in music.

- Neil Kinnock, former leader of the Labour Party, was fond of pointing out that he was the first person in his family to go to university, not because his predecessors were not necessarily incapable of learning, but because the opportunity was not available to them.

Given these facts, we need to recognize that people can often learn and change, but some things about them are pretty well fixed and we must work within the constraints that this imposes.

Individual personalities

In Chapter 3 we saw that personality consisted of five different dimensions:

- *Neuroticism* – how easily we respond to the world around us – our emotional stability. Some people get upset or angry very easily, others will be very stable.

- *Extraversion* – how much people enjoy being with other people and being actively engaged with them or how much they prefer to be on their own or with small intimate groups (introverts).

- *Openness* to different interests – people with a high level of openness will do lots of things and be very inquisitive, but not examine things in as much depth as people with a low openness who will be highly involved with few interests.

- *Agreeableness* – how accommodating we are to alternative attitudes, values and points of view. People who are most accommodating will accept a wide range, whereas those who are least accommodating will tend to have strong opinions and not listen to others.

- *Conscientiousness* – how committed and organized we are to do something. People who are very conscientious will get on and do what they say they are going to do, whereas people who are not conscientious can be unreliable.

It is generally believed that many of these characteristics are also hard-wired, but that they can be affected by our early experiences, either encouraging or discouraging certain tendencies. So, people who have a tendency to be more or less neurotic may be made more so or less so by their early family circumstances, but the tendency will not be completely reversed. It is a bit like a TV set that may automatically find stations but then can be fine-tuned to the best picture.

As we get older these tendencies become more fixed and are harder to affect, except in very small ways. It is no use expecting someone who has a few, very intense, interests or who is very fixed in their ways to change radically once they reach adulthood. On the other hand, do not assume that these are the characteristics of older people, and that younger people are by nature more 'open' or 'agreeable'. The reality is that most people tend towards the middle of the range on each of these dimensions (Figure 7.1).

Two things to note:

1 There is no clear evidence that people tend towards particular combinations of personality (introverts are no more likely to be neurotic than to be stable), so that each person has their own combination of personality traits.

2 Just because someone has a very extreme personality trait on one dimension does not mean that they will be at one extreme or another on any of the others.

If you want to get the best out of someone you need to understand their personality. This does not mean getting everyone to

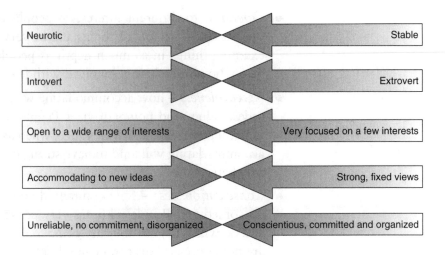

Figure 7.1   People tend towards the middle of the personality dimensions

take a personality test, but simply being alert to each person's characteristics and recognizing the implications.

- Some people will tend to be more emotional or get more anxious about events; others may seem unmoved by circumstances that would cause most people to react very strongly. You need to learn to judge people's reaction individually, and distinguish their reactions so that you recognize how each is affected.

- Some people make friends easily, enjoy the limelight and seize every opportunity to be the centre of attention, while others keep themselves to themselves and find being asked to speak in a group or stand out from the crowd quite stressful. On the one hand, you need to make sure that the extroverts do not hog all your attention or dominate discussions and ensure the introverts are not isolated and alone and are able to make a contribution to the work of the team or workgroup.

- It is useful having people who are willing to specialize and become experts in one or two areas, and you should harness their enthusiasm to ensure that you can draw on that depth of knowledge and skill. Equally, it is also useful to have people who can turn their hand to many things, giving you more flexibility.

- One of the challenges of leadership – perhaps the defining characteristic of effective leaders – is the ability to make change happen successfully. Having people who are open to new ideas makes this easier, whereas people with strong, fixed views can be a real barrier to change. However, there are few people who are so fixed that they cannot change and, once they have been convinced of the arguments for change, those who were most reluctant to accept the new ideas can often become the strongest advocates for them.

- Some people have real problems keeping organized, are unreliable and lack commitment. As a leader you will need to pay extra attention to them, helping them to manage their work, giving them a more rigid structure to work in maybe, and monitoring their progress and encouraging them to be more committed. Others need far less attention because they just get on with things, do what they say they will do and are highly dedicated.

The real challenge for leaders is to recognize these differences and adjust your leadership behaviour to match their individual personalities, without seeming to have favourites or to ignore people. Far too many managers fail as leaders because they think that treating people equally means treating everybody the same when, in fact, it means treating them fairly without favouritism but in accordance with their specific needs. It also means making sure that you do not ignore (or seem to ignore) those people who need less attention because they are able to cope alone, get on with things without making a song and dance about it, and accept changes without too much resistance. The best leaders are aware of everyone's contribution and make sure that people know that they are aware. This means:

- Being observant, always being alert to what people are doing and recognizing their emotional responses (whether they are happy or sad, enthusiastic or reluctant, etc.). This is what is meant by *emotional intelligence*, an important skill for leaders to develop, as we saw in Chapter 3.

- Acknowledging and thanking them for what they do, both publicly and privately, from time to time. People like deserved praise (although they may not always agree what is deserved and what is not!) and leaders are always willing to give it when they think it is deserved.

- Equally, if someone has not performed to the expected standard when they are capable of doing so, then you should not ignore that either. However, that should nearly always be done in private and should be used as an opportunity to work out how it can be done better in future, not simply for you to express your anger or dismay.

- Suiting the tasks you ask people to do to their abilities and personalities, while also stretching people by taking them out of their comfort zone (but not too far). The introvert who is asked to buddy a new employee or the person who is reluctant to change being given responsibility for a component of a change programme can help people overcome some of their natural inclinations.

First line or middle managers who want to be effective leaders have to know well the people they lead. Treating people as individuals means putting time and effort into getting to know and understand them as individual personalities and using this knowledge to shape their behaviour.

Diversity

The word diversity is used very loosely, but it is meant to emphasize that the UK, like most Western European countries, is no longer a homogeneous society (if it ever was). The workforce contains men and women of different ages, different religious beliefs, different ethnic backgrounds and with different physical abilities, marital and family relationships and sexuality. There is legal protection of most of these dimensions of diversity, but this book is less concerned with these, and far more concerned about the way that your leadership performance is affected by leading a diverse group of people.

Clearly, an effective leader should be aware of and observe the legal requirements that govern workplace behaviour. Any competent manager should know and understand what the law requires and the obligations this places on organizations and managers. However, there is a difference between abiding by the letter of the law, and observing it in spirit. More significantly, ensuring that people are able to work to their full potential means that all the potential barriers to them doing so are removed and that they are offered real equality of opportunity. In return for ensuring that people are treated fairly and equally and that their differences are recognized and welcomed, you then have the right to expect that everyone you lead makes the same level of commitment to working to their full potential.

What does this mean in practice? It means:

- Recognizing that people may have particular wishes or needs that derive from their religion (the opportunity to attend services at particular times, for example), their physical disabilities (the need to use particular equipment, for example) or family circumstances (a parent's need to cope with children's illness, for example). This does not mean giving people special treatment, simply looking at ways in which work patterns or tasks can be organized to enable them to do what they have to do, while ensuring that the work gets done efficiently and effectively (which is what really matters).

● Acknowledge your own ignorance. Do not hide what you do not know about a disability or a religion, but show interest and (without prying) encourage people to tell you about themselves and any specific wishes or needs they may have. This is a good opportunity to demonstrate your communication skills and emotional intelligence, finding things out with sensitivity.

● Not tolerating language or behaviour that is divisive or verging towards being discriminatory. This means making it clear that such language or behaviour is not acceptable, wherever or whenever it is used. You should also explain why it is not acceptable, not simply because it is – or is heading towards being – illegal, but because it is offensive to you personally and because it breaks the 'golden rule'. (Do you remember that, from Chapter 2? Nobody should treat others in ways that they would not want to be treated themselves.)

Leadership in a diverse society is not about being 'politically correct' because that just means going through the motions of seeming to treat people equally. It is about treating each person on the same terms, not trying to offend and being sensitive to words or behaviours that offend unintentionally. Above all, it means showing respect for others, in return for which they will respect you.

Individual abilities

People have different sets of knowledge and skills. Even when they have had the same education, training and work experience (and very few people will have identical backgrounds), they will still perform differently at the same tasks. A leader needs to know what each person is capable of doing, what they need to learn or what experience they need, and what they are capable of helping others to learn.

A good way of doing this is to use a *skills matrix* to record what skills people have and what tasks they are capable of performing. A skills matrix is simply a table with the people you lead listed down the side and all the tasks they may need to perform along

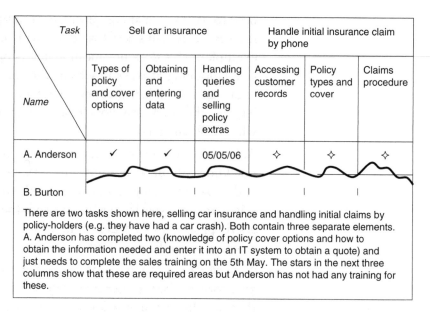

Task / Name	Sell car insurance			Handle initial insurance claim by phone		
	Types of policy and cover options	Obtaining and entering data	Handling queries and selling policy extras	Accessing customer records	Policy types and cover	Claims procedure
A. Anderson	✓	✓	05/05/06	✧	✧	✧
B. Burton						

There are two tasks shown here, selling car insurance and handling initial claims by policy-holders (e.g. they have had a car crash). Both contain three separate elements. A. Anderson has completed two (knowledge of policy cover options and how to obtain the information needed and enter it into an IT system to obtain a quote) and just needs to complete the sales training on the 5th May. The stars in the next three columns show that these are required areas but Anderson has not had any training for these.

Figure 7.2 A skills matrix (car insurance call centre)

the top (Figure 7.2). If necessary, larger tasks may be broken down into their components, to reflect the knowledge, skills and experience – or *competence* – required.

The value of a skills matrix is that it helps you to allocate tasks to individuals in line with their competence and also provides you with a mechanism to manage their development. The more people you lead, the harder this is without a record or a plan, which is what the skills matrix offers. People are motivated by opportunities to learn and develop their competence; a skills matrix provides a structured analysis of what each person is capable of doing plus clear, planned opportunities for them to develop and improve, to maximize the motivational effect.

It is important to remember that training and development are a key part of performance improvement, but that does not mean it should be used as reward for good performance or as an alternative to dealing with serious performance problems.

- If someone has mastered a particular task and is ready to move on to something new, that is one thing, but giving someone two days' training as a reward for having worked hard tells everyone that training is not important, it is just a day off work.

- If someone is messing about at work, arriving late or not applying themselves to the task, your first task is to find out why. Is it because they are not competent, or is it a lack of commitment or family problems? Training only solves problems with knowledge or skills, not a poor attitude or parental divorce. Too many managers avoid dealing with such issues by passing the problem on to trainers to solve; leaders address the real problem.

Key idea

Competence

The word competence has been used a lot in training and development circles over the last 20 years or so, and is used in the UK to mean:

The ability to perform a task to the standard required in employment.

Competence is about more than simply being able to repeat a series of actions in rote form, like a robot that has been programmed to do the same thing, time after time, in exactly the same way. People have hands, arms and legs, but they also have brains and competence involves using those brains.

Competence depends on three elements:

1 *Knowledge*, of facts and theories, procedures and principles, so that people know what to do and why. In more advanced jobs this knowledge may be very complex, in others it is very straightforward and matter of fact, but all tasks require some knowledge, however basic it may be.

2 *Skills*, both practical ones (the ability to perform physical tasks in the appropriate way) and mental ones (the ability to make complex decisions or recognize how people are reacting to what you say to them).

3 *Experience* in the job, learning how the different bits of knowledge and skills fit together in the real world, what practical judgements need to be made and how to balance different pressures (such as cost versus quality).

It is the combination of these three that enables people to become competent. There is a long tradition of people having to undertake formal training (to acquire knowledge and skills) and work experience (to develop their ability to use what they have learned) in order to become competent in their jobs. This includes apprenticeships, 'articled clerks' (for solicitors and accountants) and 'housemen' (for trainee doctors).

Knowledge and skills can be taught on the job or off, but experience can only be acquired by doing the work. Leaders are always keen to encourage people to stretch themselves by doing new things, while ensuring that they do not get over-stretched. This means monitoring closely when someone does something new, or making sure that another team member does. Getting others to *mentor* (guide and support) a person doing something new provides two development opportunities:

- learners get experience of something new
- mentors learn how to pass on their knowledge and experience and gain further confidence.

Leaders do not try to do everything for themselves but look at every task and judge:

- Who can do it best?
- Who needs to improve their performance in this task?
- Who could help someone else to learn how to perform the task?
- How urgent and important is the task?
- How many people can currently perform the task?
- How many people should be able to perform the task?

There are no rules for deciding what to do; you must make a judgement based on your own knowledge and experience. Leadership rarely operates by set rules.

Individual learning styles

We saw in Chapter 4 that people may tend to have different abilities (what Howard Gardner has called 'multiple intelligences') and, in Chapter 5, that people seem to have different preferences in how they learn. You need to be alert to these differences and their effects on people's behaviour and task performance (how they do the jobs they do). For example (according to David Kolb):

- *Divergers* will often use their experience to develop their performance, looking for ways to use any new skills they have acquired. They are likely to be good at putting forward ideas for improving processes and trying out new ways of working.

- *Assimilators* will be concerned with why things are the way they are, the reasons for each task and the procedure for performing the task. Until that is all clear, they will be reluctant or very cautious about doing anything new.

- *Accommodators* will be keen to try new things without necessarily having the necessary competence, and will be reluctant to spend time developing their knowledge and skills. They do not always look at the consequences of their actions; however, they are always willing to have a go and will not be put off by anything new.

- *Convergers* are good at dealing with the unexpected and taking risks, trying things out and adapting their plans in the light of the outcomes, although they might benefit from reflecting afterwards about events and learning from their experience.

Your job as a leader is to:

1 recognize these differences

2 draw on people's strengths by suiting the tasks you allocate to the person, but also

3 encourage people to develop and improve their performance by encouraging them to address any weaknesses that result from their learning style.

This means getting:

- *divergers* to think about why things are done as they are, or why they should be changed, and not just dive in without any thought

- *assimilators* to think about how what they know should affect how they perform, what practical skills and behaviour they need, as well as theories and principles they have learned

- *accommodators* to reflect on what happened as a result of what they did, and how they might use this knowledge to improve their performance in future

- *convergers* to consider why things happened the way they did and to be alert to the underlying causes so that they can plan better for the future.

The art of leadership (and it is an art rather than a science) is being sensitive to individuals and treating each person differently in line with their abilities.

Setting individual objectives

In Chapter 4 we mentioned SMART objectives and emphasized that it was more important for leaders to set the direction and values for the group of people they lead. However, individuals do need a more specific set of goals, and this can mean agreeing SMART goals. However, before looking at what that involves, let us just think about the role that goals or objectives play.

Reflection

- Do you have any goals or objectives, either personal ones or work ones?

- How were they set, how is performance monitored, and how are your goals or objectives reviewed and changed?

- Do the people you lead have goals or objectives?

- How are they set, how is performance monitored, and how are these goals or objectives reviewed and changed?

Think about your answers as you read the next section of *Introducing Leadership*.

Words like aims, objectives, targets and goals tend to be used interchangeably. For simplicity, we are going to use them with a very specific set of meanings. Aims, objectives and targets will all be classed as 'goals' with the meanings shown in Figure 7.3.

Goals	Meaning
Aims	Very broad and general, not all that specific; set for the longer term and likely to change only very gradually over time, as the goal shifts slightly one way or another. In the terms we used earlier, aims are the general direction being headed for.
Objectives	Specific and focused on achievement in the medium term, with performance measured and the objectives reviewed periodically, to check that they are still correct and achievable.
Targets	Very specific, shorter-term goals that contribute to the achievement of objectives, which are monitored but are unlikely to be changed unless something significant happens to prevent them being achieved or to make them no longer relevant.

Figure 7.3 Goals

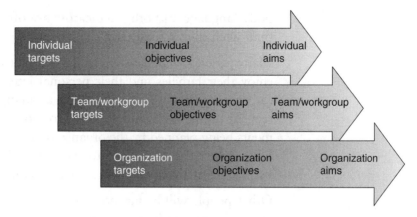

Figure 7.4 Aligning goals

The idea is that targets are steps towards objectives which move you towards your aims. The further away they are, the less specific the goals and the longer the timescale over which they should be set. By agreeing targets and objectives with individuals you can help people fulfil their personal goals in life (aims) and also ensure that the organization's and the team's or workgroup's goals are achieved (Figure 7.4). There is more about the team's or workgroup's goals in Chapter 8.

Individual aims

People all have different aims in their lives. Some people will be very job focused and look forward to a high-flying career, while others have a focus more on their family, their hobby or pastime, or their political, religious or community commitments. These different focuses will shape their personal aims, although most people will want to achieve something in all these different roles that they play (employee, parent, hobbyist and committee member).

You need to be alert to each person's individual aims in life. You can discuss them as part of a formal performance appraisal system (although appraisal meetings do not often have enough time for such longer-term thinking), but the best way to learn what each person is aiming for is to talk to them informally and listen carefully to what they say. It is not about asking 'What do you want to do with your life?', but observing and thinking about an individual's day-to-day conversations and behaviour. (In Chapter 4 we talked about communication skills and the way that people communicate with much more then their words – their tone of voice, body language and other indicators are often far more important than what they actually say.)

Many people will be satisfied with a quiet life and the opportunity to enjoy their families and their personal interests, with very limited career aims. Do not treat such people as unimportant; they also want security in their jobs, and you need to show them how any developments being planned by the organization can offer this – not by stability (which can easily lead to eventual decline and insecurity) but by planned change and responsiveness to the changing environment.

Other people will be far more goal-oriented, although those goals may not necessarily obviously be aligned with the organization's. They may have environmental concerns and be keen to do something about ecological or climate threats. Others will be concerned about world poverty or research into debilitating or deadly diseases. If your organization has a policy on waste or environmental protection, corporate social responsibility or a community support programme, these can provide a vehicle for harnessing people's commitment by encouraging them to become involved in activities designed to implement these policies.

Of course, there will also be people whose primary goals are to develop their careers, to move on and up in this or another organization. You should be aware of these goals and look at opportunities to support them if at all possible, if that will enable the organization to grow and develop as well. This might mean encouraging such people to take up opportunities for training and development that will enable them to achieve their goals, or to gain experience of working in new areas.

One of the great myths that far too many managers believe in is that training people wastes money because, once trained, people leave for better jobs elsewhere. The evidence is to the contrary – organizations that invest in training tend not only to retain staff, but attract better, more committed staff in the first place. Leaders understand this. They recognize that a successful organization is one that cares for the people it employs and that, in return, they will care for it. This mutual respect for each other, employer and employee, creates an environment in which people are willing to be led.

Richard Branson was once asked who was most important to him in his Virgin empire – shareholders, customers or employees. He was quite clear, it was employees because, if he cared about his employees, they would care about the customers and that would keep the shareholders happy. First line and middle managers are the people who are closest to the people they lead, and are best able to be aware of what they want out of life, individually. By caring about them and their goals they will produce better products or services, more efficiently, ensuring the organization meets its goals.

Individual objectives

Most formal performance management or appraisal systems involve agreeing specific objectives with individuals; these are often (but not always) expressed as SMART objectives (Figure 7.5).

S	Specific – as opposed to being vague or unclear
M	Measurable – so that it is possible to tell when they have been achieved
A	Achievable – so that people are not being set impossible goals, and are set up to fail
R	Resourced – so that the equipment, materials or money needed to make the objectives achievable are available
T	Timed – so that there are clear dates for the achievement of the objectives

NB: There are variants in the meanings given to the letters but their effect is the same, they just say the same things in slightly different ways.

Figure 7.5 SMART objectives

While there is nothing wrong with the idea, in principle, the practice associated with such objective setting and review can present problems. For a start, the need to be able to measure performance against objectives means, by definition, that only those objectives that can be measured get agreed. There is also an inbuilt tendency for the process of objective setting to become a conflict between two opponents, one trying to set objectives as high as possible, the other as low, a bit like bartering in a marketplace. Third, the emphasis on objectives shifts attention from *how* people work to *what* they achieve, which does not focus on what people need to do to improve. Finally, the need to go through a formal process of objective setting and review means that too much emphasis is placed on getting it done, when the most important thing is what someone is actually doing in their job. These four aspects of performance review:

1 focusing only on the measurable

2 competitive bartering (looking for win:lose) rather than collaborative discussion (win:win)

3 focusing on outcomes not processes

4 getting the bureaucracy right not the person

are not inevitable, but they are common. Leadership means focusing on the person, how they work with other people and the tasks they have to perform; this is a significant feature of what John Adair has called Action Centred Leadership. Adair argues that leadership is primarily concerned with ensuring that people, teams and tasks are aligned to best effect. That means making sure that people are able to play an active part in the team and work with others, while also ensuring that tasks are allocated to the right person and completed effectively.

To do this well you have to be alert to how individuals and teams are performing tasks on a day-to-day basis. A performance management system that involves sitting down every three, six or 12 months to set objectives and review performance does not encourage managers to treat employees as individuals, some of whom would benefit from much more regular review, or to recognize that tasks may have different timescales or that priorities may change. The worst feature of performance management systems is that they are used to judge individual's suitability for financial rewards. Even worse, when the rewards are limited, it does not matter how well someone performs but how well they perform in relation to others. If people are supposed to be working in teams yet some will get rewards when others will not, this runs counter to the whole idea of teamworking.

Is there an alternative? There is, but it is far less structured, more individual and dependent on the skills and integrity of the leader. This makes it difficult for larger organizations to cope with, because they prefer standardized procedures that are not dependent on the personal qualities of the person operating them. This approach involves:

- Agreeing objectives for individuals that look at all aspects of what they do and include some that are important but hard or subjective to measure ('Getting more enjoyment from my work'; 'Create better relationships with customers/suppliers/ fellow team members').

- Monitor how well people are performing constantly but not by being overbearing. Do it by showing interest in their progress, helping them if they are stuck and praising them when they are doing well. Encourage them to self-monitor so that they achieve their objectives because they want to, not because you are checking up on them.

- Use timescales for formal reviews of individuals that relate to their own needs or preferences and to their work cycle, not an artificial timescale that suits organizational tidiness. Some people need frequent review because they lack confidence in what they are doing or are doing something new and need to be certain they are heading in the right direction. Others may be working consistently and confidently, perhaps as part of a team so that their individual performance is only part of a larger whole which can more easily be monitored. They benefit from regular informal reviews, but a formal process is not really necessary or useful.

Of course, your employer may have formal systems that you have to follow. That does not stop you operating an informal system alongside to enable you to ensure that the people you lead get the support and encouragement they need.

Individual targets

Targets are short-term goals, sometimes called milestones because they measure progress towards our ultimate goal. Targets can be invaluable in helping individuals to achieve agreed objectives, as they provide a *feedback loop*, confirming when they are on target or helping to re-adjust to get back on target.

Key idea

Feedback loop

A feedback loop is a very common feature of systems; one we all come into contact with in cold weather is a thermostat:

- you set the desired temperature (*the target*)
- a thermometer measures the actual temperature and compares it to the desired temperature (*monitoring*)
- if the temperature is above target it shuts the heating off; if it is below target it turns it on (*action*).

Feedback loops are simply ways of monitoring performance and making changes as a result. It is the 'making changes' which is the important part. Without any monitoring (and it should always be the simplest and quickest, to avoid wasting time and resources) then people do not know how they are doing. But monitoring on its own is not enough, it has to be matched by goals (to have something against which to judge performance) and a readiness to change, if necessary, to get back on course.

Figure 7.6 shows what happens if people do not have targets against which to measure progress towards their objectives. The longer the timescale over which the objectives have been set, the further off course they can get.

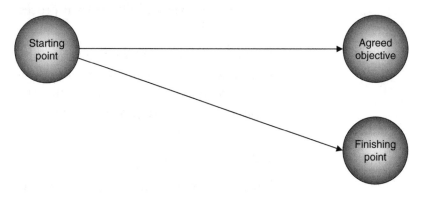

Figure 7.6   Objectives without targets

But targets, which create intermediate steps along the way, can provide opportunities to monitor progress and correct the direction, bringing people back on course (Figure 7.7).

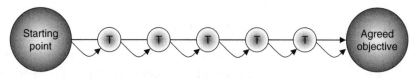

Figure 7.7   Objectives with targets

Of course, nothing is quite as easy as this makes it look, but the principle is the important thing. Targets can be set one-by-one, as each is achieved, providing a short-term goal to move people forward. They can also help if the final objective has to be changed in the light of experience. For example:

● The reasons for setting that objective have changed, and a new direction needs to be set.

- It is clear that the original objective was over-ambitious and needs to be scaled back, or was too easy and is not stretching the person enough.

It is important to recognize that just because a target has been set, it is not cast in stone. Targets are designed to focus on the desired performance and not because, in themselves, they are important. And one final point to remember about targets – they can also help to motivate people, something we will look at soon.

Individual feedback

As we have seen, feedback on performance is critical in enabling people to achieve their objectives and improve their performance. However, feedback has to be done properly if it is to be effective, and that means suiting the feedback to the person and the cause. Feedback can be used to:

- recognize good performance, to encourage that person to maintain the standard
- acknowledge hard work or effort (which may not have resulted in high levels of performance, but still needs to be recognized)
- help to improve poor performance by advising an individual or suggesting training and development activity
- explore reasons for low levels of effort, to demonstrate your concern about someone's commitment.

You will notice that there is a difference between good or poor performance due to levels of competence (knowledge, skill and experience) and good or poor performance due to lack of effort or commitment. It is important to make this distinction because it stems from very different causes. If I can work well but choose not to I may be feeling unhappy or depressed due to personal or work problems, or I may have decided that this is not the job for me. There could also be changes at work that are causing me to be dissatisfied (new shift patterns or bonus schemes). On the other hand, if I cannot do the job it may be due to poor induction or training or a fault in the recruitment process (not defining the requirements properly).

Your role is to identify the causes by observing, asking questions and listening to individuals, then providing the appropriate feedback. In giving feedback it is useful to remember the acronym *U-STAR* ('You star!' – see Figure 7.8).

U	Understandable	It is no good giving feedback in language that cannot be understood, so it is important to check that people know why they did well or badly and what needs to be done either to repeat it (if it was good) or improve it (if it was bad)
S	Specific	Make sure that people understand what aspects of their performance you are referring to and why it was good or needs improving
T	Timely	Feedback should be given as soon as possible after the performance it refers to, in order to have maximum effect
A	Accurate	Make sure you feedback to the person who was actually responsible and in relation to what they actually did – it may seem obvious, but too often people are praised for something someone else did, or for something completely different from what they did
R	Relevant	Feedback should help people sustain good perform-ance or improve poor performance, and different people respond to feedback in different ways. Only by knowing the people you lead can you judge how people will respond to feedback and provide it to them in ways that are relevant to them, as individuals

Figure 7.8   Giving feedback

At the heart of good feedback is awareness of what people are doing. Leaders do not sit in offices reading reports, they wander round observing what is happening. When things go well or badly they find out how and why. Only by knowing why things have gone well or badly can you do something about it, and only by know-ing the people you lead can you identify their role and responsi-bility, their personality and ability, and provide feedback that is right for them.

Individual motivation

What makes people really want to achieve their goals? Some people will try as hard as they can to get where they want to go, while others will give up at the first hurdle. The simple answer is moti-vation, but that just gives a name to it, it does not explain the process. If you are to lead people effectively you need to know what will make them want to follow you. The best way of doing this is to head towards the goals that you have agreed with them. If people want to go in a particular direction, to head towards a particular objective and to reach a series of targets, because those are goals that they want to achieve, then they will follow you if you look likely to lead them towards them. But it still does not explain why people want to move in that direction and want to follow you. That is why we need to understand motivation.

One of the most popular explanations for motivation was developed by Abraham Maslow, something that we looked at in Chapter 3. His idea, that we have a hierarchy of needs from the basic physiological, through safety, love and esteem to self-actualization (see Figure 3.3, p. 54), may explain our general, everyday behaviour, but is too crude to be used easily to motivate individuals, other than to emphasize that people are not keen to work in unhealthy, unsafe, unwelcoming environments where they are treated badly and not developed.

Frederick Herzberg's distinction between hygiene factors (which demotivate us if they are not present – see Figure 3.4, p. 54) and the drivers which actually motivate us is a more useful approach. It encourages you to look at the conditions of employment and check that the hygiene factors have been satisfied before looking at what you can do to motivate people. Adrian Furnham, Professor of Occupational Psychology at University College London, argues that the most important motivational factors are, in order of importance:

1 the intrinsic value of the job (making sure that jobs are interesting)

2 being given responsibility (such as the authority to make decisions and responsibility for tasks such as mentoring or training others)

3 giving feedback and creating a sense of achievement (recognizing performance by an occasional pat on the back or publicly celebrating individual or team achievement, and by suggesting how people can learn and improve)

4 providing training and development opportunities (to enable career progression and ensure that people are good at doing the things they are employed to do)

5 showing people respect (when talking to them and involving them in decisions).

The other theory of motivation that we mentioned in Chapter 3 was Reversal Theory. This is a very practical theory of motivation and can be used to help you recognize the state that an individual is in and how that is affecting their performance. The four pairs of opposite states are listed in Figure 7.9, with guidance on how

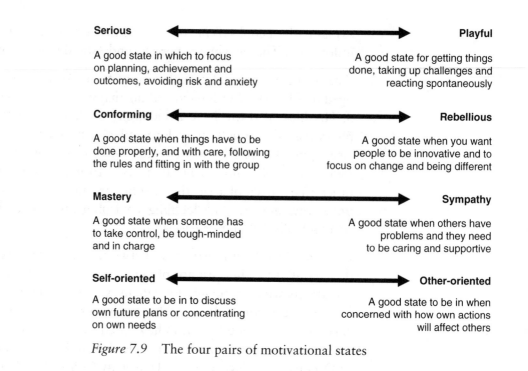

Serious ⟷ **Playful**

A good state in which to focus on planning, achievement and outcomes, avoiding risk and anxiety

A good state for getting things done, taking up challenges and reacting spontaneously

Conforming ⟷ **Rebellious**

A good state when things have to be done properly, and with care, following the rules and fitting in with the group

A good state when you want people to be innovative and to focus on change and being different

Mastery ⟷ **Sympathy**

A good state when someone has to take control, be tough-minded and in charge

A good state when others have problems and they need to be caring and supportive

Self-oriented ⟷ **Other-oriented**

A good state to be in to discuss own future plans or concentrating on own needs

A good state to be in when concerned with how own actions will affect others

Figure 7.9   The four pairs of motivational states

you can use this to best effect. The key thing to remember is that people tend to have preferences between pairs but that we can all operate in one or the other state, and that we will be in one or other of each pair at all times.

If you are trying to plan and the person you are working with just wants to get on with the task, then they are going to be in the wrong motivational state (they will not be interested in planning or looking to the future but are in a *playful* state). If the person is constantly arguing: 'That's not the way that things have to be done' when you are trying to generate innovative ideas, then they are in the wrong motivational state (they are *conforming*). If you have asked someone to coach another and all they do is take over, they are in the wrong motivational state (they are motivated by *mastery*), and if someone has got real problems and another member of the team is only concerned about his or her own needs, they are in the wrong motivational state (*self-* not *other-oriented*).

Some people tend to be dominant in one or other of a pair of these motivational states. This means that they will more often be in that state than the other of that pair. It does not mean that they cannot be in the other state, but it is less likely. You should recognize this and look out for occasions when they switch to the other state and ask yourself, 'What caused that? What has happened that seems to have made them switch?' You can use this to create situations that produce the desired motivational state to help you achieve the outcomes you are looking for.

Reversal theory sounds quite complex, and some aspects are, but the basic idea:

- that we have four pairs of states (*Serious/Playful, Conforming/Rebellious, Mastery/Sympathy* and *Self-oriented/Other-oriented*)
- that we switch from one to another of each pair at different times
- that we will be in one of each pair at all times

is useful in allowing you to make sense of how different people respond to the same situation in different ways, and the same person responds differently at different times. Our motivational state varies and the challenge for leaders is to recognize how each individual behaves and use this to bring about the outcomes you want.

Summary

- Leadership, especially at first line and middle management level, is all about understanding people as individuals in an incredibly diverse society. This means recognizing that each person is different and understanding those individual differences, whether it is due to personality, ability or some other characteristic.

- Some aspects of our difference are hard-wired, whether it is our personality or our physical or mental abilities, others are learned from our birth and throughout our lives. Leaders need to be alert to what is fixed (and work with those features) and what can be changed (and take advantage of opportunities to develop people).

- Objectives and targets can be used to help people achieve their personal and the organizational goals and fulfil their potential. Leaders have responsibility for agreeing goals with people and ensuring that these goals reflect what is important, not just what can be easily measured and fits into formal systems. Regular feedback, and review of performance and progress are essential if people are to perform consistently to the highest standards.

GETTING THE BEST OUT OF INDIVIDUALS

- Feedback needs to be understandable, specific, timely, accurate and relevant to the individual (U-STAR) and will only have these characteristics if leaders know well the people they lead and suit their feedback to the person.

- Leaders need to understand what motivates individuals and use this to get the best out of them. Because we are all different we respond differently to different things, and leaders should tailor their behaviour to motivate each person individually.

8 Getting the best out of groups and teams

Workplaces these days are full of teams – or to be precise, are organized into workgroups called teams. In fact, there is far more to teams and teamworking than simply taking a group of people, giving them a day's 'team-building' activity and renaming them as a team. In this chapter we will look at the difference between 'groups' and 'teams', at the role of leadership in effective group and team-working, and what first line and middle managers can do to help build their workgroups into effective teams.

Working in groups

People are naturally gregarious – in the main, they like being with other people. Of course, being gregarious is one aspect of our personality, in particular of our degree of extraversion or introversion, so that extreme extroverts need company, extreme introverts avoid it, and the majority (who are clustered midway between the two) like some company most of the time. Some evolutionary psychologists argue that working in groups is part of our genetic background. As humans evolved they learned that working cooperatively was more productive than working in isolation and so those who were more gregarious prospered.

Division of labour and scientific management

You do not have to accept evolutionary psychologists' argument to acknowledge that group working has its advantages. Adam Smith wrote what is often regarded as the founding book of the study of economics, *The Wealth of Nations*, in which he described how modern manufacturing had developed the idea of *division of labour* (Figure 8.1). Division of labour had always existed, as different people had specialized in different types of work (farmer, baker, blacksmith, etc.) for centuries, but what Smith described was the way this was being carried through into the newly emerging factories,

'One man draws out the wire, another straights it, a third cuts it, a fourth points it, a fifth grinds it at the top for receiving the head; to make the head requires two or three distinct operations; to put it on is a peculiar business, to whiten the pins is another; it is even a trade by itself to put them into the paper; and the important business of making a pin is, in this manner, divided into about eighteen distinct operations, which, in some factories, are all performed by distinct hands, though in others the same man will sometimes perform two or three of them.'

From: Adam Smith, *An Inquiry into the Nature and Causes of the Wealth of Nations* (1776)

Figure 8.1   Pin-making

where each broad occupation was subdivided into separate tasks carried out by groups of workers.

What makes this so significant is not just that people are working cooperatively in groups, although that is an essential component of division of labour, but that someone else has organized their work, buying different machines and setting up a workflow so that the output of one man's work becomes the input of the next. Factories were largely an 18th century invention and changed nearly all work activity from individual (with perhaps a few employees) to group working. Within 150 years, the simple processes described by Smith had evolved into the factory that Henry Ford built on the banks of the Rouge River in Dearborn, Michigan, between 1917 and 1925. Ford's revolutionary manufacturing complex turned raw materials into finished cars all on one site. Ford's *vertically integrated* approach (uniting all phases of the production process under one roof) combined division of labour with *standardization* (using standard parts in all vehicles, with little or no variation in models) and the economies of very large-scale production to bring about dramatic reductions in unit costs. In 1908 (before the new plant was built), Ford produced 27 Model T cars a day and sold them for over $800 each. By 1923, 2000 cars were rolling off the production line every day and selling for $395 each.

However, the average employee left after 3 months. This was not due to poor wages – Ford paid above average, especially as the company employed relatively unskilled people – but was generally because people found the work overpowering. Individual decision-making had been replaced by managerial control, eliminating freedom of action. This was largely due to the influence of American *scientific management* theorist FW Taylor[1], who is generally regarded as the founder of *work study*. Taylor believed that people should not be allowed to design their own work methods, that through careful study and analysis, scientific management could design more efficient and effective ways of doing the job.

Reflection

How do you feel about Taylor's approach? How much freedom do people in your organization have to design their own work methods? If they are largely designed by managers, how 'scientific' are their methods of doing so?

Taylor (and Ford) removed all responsibility for how the job would be done. Each employee was expected to undertake a sequence of tasks in a prescribed way, and paid largely on the basis of output (*piece rates*). There is a lot of evidence that such approaches have real benefits, for organizations and employees alike. Modern ergonomics has led to the major redesign of workflow systems, equipment and procedures to improve efficiency and effectiveness, and has reduced the risks of injury, for example in the handling of heavy objects. Taylor's scientific management pioneered studies on how tasks can best be performed, with less emphasis on the health and safety risks and more on economics but, nevertheless, he valued safety if only because accidents could stop the line.

The principles of mass production have been applied to service industries in recent years, and the growth of call centres in the latter part of the 20th century has been likened to the growth of car plants in the early decades. Just as division of labour was accelerated by the new technology of steam and then electric power, so mass production in services has been accelerated by the development of information and communications technology (ICT). It is impossible to separate out the way people work from the technology that they use but, as technology has evolved, it has meant that some of the characteristics of early mass production, such as standardization and large-scale production are not necessarily as relevant, as we will see below.

From reducing cost to improving quality

The growth of mass production was all about cutting costs, as Ford showed with the price of the Model T, but it also relied on standardization, on machines and employees churning out identical parts and assembling them in identical ways. Unfortunately, both people and machines are fallible; they wear out and make mistakes. That is why Taylor insisted on tight supervision to control workers, but that kind of managerial control caused dissatisfaction and led to car unions being some of the most militant across the world.

In the post-war years, factories in Japan, rebuilding its economy after the destruction wrought by World War II, started to use techniques that were taught to them by two American engineers, W. Edwards Deming and Joseph Juran. These techniques were first developed in the USA during the war to help improve the production of weapons (which needed high quality as well as mass production) and, at the heart of these developments, was the return of some responsibility to the workforce. There is more about this in Chapter 10, but for the moment we will focus on one aspect of it, the movement towards group working, because the 'quality revolution' has centred on the role that workgroups play in quality control and quality improvement.

As we saw in Chapter 4, James Surowiecki has argued (in *The Wisdom of Crowds*, Little, Brown: 2004) that groups of people make better decisions than individuals. It was this that led to the use of workgroups as the basis for improvement. Instead of managers designing work tasks and tightly controlling what individuals did, the role shifted to their being responsible for leading workgroups through the process of:

1 monitoring their own work, based on agreed standards

2 identifying problems and their causes

3 developing solutions to these problems

4 implementing the new ways of working.

People prefer working in groups and taking responsibility for the group's work because it reflects our general personalities (as mildly extrovert) and our desire to have some control over our own lives. In return, employers get better motivated workforces and are able to use the knowledge and experience (the 'wisdom') of their employees to solve problems and make changes that are most likely to work.

Of course, it does not always work. There are some jobs that cannot easily be divided up within a group and some people who prefer working on their own. Organizations should not try to use group working everywhere simply because it works well in most cases, nor should they expect everyone to be a natural group worker. The challenge is to recognize which is which. Modern personality tests are good at picking out the individual who prefers to work alone; tasks that are best undertaken by individuals. include those that have some of the following criteria:

- Tasks that do not divide up into coherent smaller tasks, but can only be completed as one task
- Tasks that demand high levels of knowledge and skill that are in short supply and/or depend upon individual flair and concentration
- Tasks that do not directly feed into, or depend directly on the output from, other tasks
- Tasks that are performed irregularly or outside the normal time patterns of group tasks.

Group working is often the best way for people to work, but that does not mean that it is always the best way, and effective managers and leaders can recognize the difference.

The challenge of leading and managing workgroups

For first line and middle managers, this emphasis on working in groups and taking on more responsibility presents real challenges. The main functions of managers – planning, organizing, commanding, coordinating and controlling – were first spelled out by Henri Fayol at much the same time as Taylor was developing his ideas about scientific management, and you can see that they have elements in common. The trouble is that encouraging groups to take more responsibility for their own work means that they do more of the planning, organizing, commanding, coordinating and controlling, so what do managers do?

For a start, managers cannot avoid responsibility for these areas. Allowing groups to organize their own work means that managers need to be able to explain the criteria that need to be observed, especially in relation to health and safety, efficiency and resource utilization, and quality. Managers also need to be alert to the requirements of other workgroups and make sure that the groups they manage do meet these requirements.

However, the most important role for managers is to provide leadership. In Chapter 1, we defined leadership as *the ability to bring about movement or change in a group or organization, when there is risk or uncertainty, by inspiring others to head in a particular direction.* Workgroups can only change the way they work, to bring about improvement, if they recognize the importance of doing so, and they must be prepared to take the risks that come with making changes. They must also make the right changes, and that means working towards the goals of the organization (direction). The leader's role is to enable workgroups to fulfil their role effectively by working with individuals (as we saw in Chapter 7) and with the group as a whole to:

- agree objectives
- ensure that the group's members have the necessary knowledge and skills
- motivate them to work together.

To do this you need to understand the dynamics of the group.

Group dynamics

What do we mean by *group dynamics*? Group dynamics is concerned with how people interact and relate to other people in the group in such a way that they influence each other's behaviour and attitudes. It reflects the fact that we do not exist in isolation from the world about us but are affected by what other people say and do, and that when we work together with others we are concerned about what they think and how they feel about us. So group dynamics is concerned with issues like:

- What is it about the group that makes people want to work cooperatively or not?
- What is it about the group that makes people want to work as hard as they can, or not (what is called 'loafing')?
- What is it about the group that makes people willing to work towards common goals?
- What is it about the group that makes people trust and respect each other?

The point is that not all groups operate effectively enough for the positive features (cooperation, commitment, common goals and mutual trust and respect) to occur. One commonly used model of how effective groups are formed was developed by Bruce Tuckman[2]. Tuckman's model suggests that groups go through a series of stages before they get to the point at which they can perform effectively:

Forming: When group members first get to know about the task they are to perform, find out about each other and test each other out

Storming: The tendency is for conflict to occur, as they fight each other over roles and responsibilities and the way that the group will work together

Norming: This third stage involves the group coming together as members start to accept each other, discuss things openly and agree their objectives and how they will work together

Performing: Now people start to occupy the roles they have agreed and undertake the tasks that they have shared between themselves

Adjourning: Sometimes labelled 'Mourning', this is the point at which a group breaks up when people often feel very emotional about the ending of the relationship between the members.

What you need to note about this model is that it describes what happens when groups are formed specifically to undertake tasks, rather than when they are formed and then reformed over time, in the way that most workgroups tend to be. Nevertheless, it does get us to focus on the significance of the relationships between group members and emphasizes the fact that there is often a lot of tension in groups, as members 'jostle for position'. This would be a problem for you, as a group leader, if it continued all the time, but the fact that it occurs occasionally should be seen as positive, as it marks periods when the group is looking at the roles and responsibilities that each member has, with a view to changing them to work better. A group that does not go through occasional upsets is possibly a group that has become a bit too passive, contented and unquestioning of its work.

What can you do to ensure that the group forms effectively? You can start by recognizing the stage it is in and asking yourself if

Forming	Make sure that they all know each other well, especially new members, both formally (their knowledge, skills and experience) and informally (their personal life, interests and pastimes).
Storming	If necessary, push people to question each other's roles and responsibilities, how tasks are allocated and undertaken. Don't be afraid of some heated debate and discussion, as long as it doesn't get too heated, to get group members to challenge the accepted way of doing things.
Norming	Make sure everyone is clear what is possible and what is not, what equipment, training and other resources are available to enable them to fulfil the roles they have agreed for each other.
Performing	Monitor relationships and be alert to any problems that are occurring. Where they reflect healthy debate and discussion, encourage people to explore possible improvements, but if there are signs of more problematic relationships, perhaps personality clashes, take action immediately to resolve them. Don't allow problems between group members to fester.
Adjourning	Encourage people to celebrate what they have achieved and then move on. Discourage people from looking back and get them focusing on the future, on new opportunities, new roles and new relationships.

Figure 8.2   Helping in group formation

this is the correct stage. Has it got stuck in one stage? Does it need help moving on or reforming? Figure 8.2 contains some advice on what you can do to help groups form more effectively.

By helping the group to form and reform, to work through these four (or five) stages you can help them to cooperate, commit themselves to the tasks that need to be completed, to work towards common goals and to trust and respect each other.

From groups to teams

So far we have talked about groups, and only about groups. Often people talk about groups and teams as if they are the same thing, but they are not. Teams are a particular type of group and there is no guarantee that any workgroup will become a team.

To start with, it is worth distinguishing between three different types of team:

1 Management teams

2 Project/*ad hoc* teams

3 Operational (product/service) teams.

152

What we are going to be talking about here is concerned with the third type, operational teams, but much of it also applies to management and project or *ad hoc* teams as well.

What makes a group a team?

What makes a team into a team is that the members see themselves as existing as a defined group (as being part of the team) and that they share some significant beliefs, ideas and values. These two features are called:

- *social identification*
- *social representation.*

'Social identification' is important, because without a strong sense that the team exists and they are part of it, people cannot feel any sense of belonging, and belonging is an important part of being a team. A workgroup is a much looser phenomenon – people know that they are part of it but that is not seen as being particularly significant for their sense of who they are as a person. Teams create a much greater degree of personal identification; people identify themselves strongly as being part of the team and see other team members as being different from everyone else (Figure 8.3).

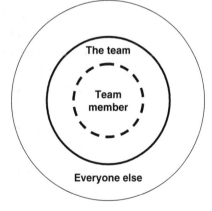

The boundaries between the individual team member and the team are thin – members feel a strong sense of identification with it – but between the team and everyone else, the boundaries are strong – the team is clearly separate from the rest of the organization, although part of it.

Figure 8.3   Being part of a team

'Social representation' means that people share certain beliefs, ideas or values that are significant for the work of the team. This does not mean that they must all have the same religion or other personal belief systems, but that they share beliefs, ideas or values in relation to issues that matter for the team. They must believe that it is important to achieve certain quality standards, not waste time or arrive late, or whatever else the other members of the team agree on.

Teamworking

What makes teamworking different from having a group of people working together as a group is that certain key essentials are in place. These are:

- That the team has a clear sense of direction, in the form of specific, hard goals coupled with feedback on the team's performance. Individual goals are set within the context of what the team is trying to achieve, and are secondary to them.
- Team members are committed to the team and to the achievement of the team's goals, particularly when put under pressure or having to face setbacks.
- The team has worked out its own ways of working together as a team and dealing with issues that may arise.

Just because the members of a group want to work as a team, it does not mean that the work they do is necessarily suitable. Teams work most effectively when the tasks they perform are complex and interdependent. That means that different people are needed to perform different functions for the whole task to be completed successfully, and that they must cooperate and collaborate to get it done. This in turn depends on the team's members having appropriate skills, in many cases that they are multi-skilled so that people can perform different tasks and substitute for each other to get the work done. Looking back at the diagram in Figure 8.2, although there are clear boundaries between the team and the rest of the organization, there are few or no boundaries between team members. They can work in different combinations and in different roles as the work demands.

If the people working together have the same skills and perform the same roles, then they are a workgroup. If they have different skills and perform different roles, if they all need to contribute to the work of the group and are prepared to switch roles and work in different combinations to do it, then they are more likely to be a team. Team members are more likely to say that this is our job, less likely to say this is my job.

For all this to happen, the organization must support teamworking. This means that work is organized in ways that enable teams to work on the complex tasks that they are best at. In the mass production approach that Ford and Taylor pioneered a century ago, organizations became very complex but tasks became very simple. Teamworking demands the opposite – simple organizations, where teams undertake complex tasks. This makes the job of first line and middle managers equally complex. Instead of allocating simple tasks to individuals, and then monitoring their performance, they must:

- agree goals for teams
- help the teams organize themselves to undertake the complex tasks
- ensure that team members have the necessary competence (knowledge, skills and experience)
- ensure that the resources required are available, maintained and effective
- remove barriers to effective teamworking and ensure that team members are able to work together effectively
- communicate to team members what is required of the team, and
- agree individual goals that enable team members to work towards the team's goals.

Leading the team becomes more important as the team becomes more self-managing, as the members take on the responsibility for planning, organizing, commanding, coordinating and controlling themselves. The benefits of teamworking are, for the team members, a better quality of working life and for the organization, improved operational performance.

The improvements in the 'quality of working life' have been shown to exist through:

- Improved employee retention and turnover rates (people stay longer in jobs they enjoy)
- Lower absence or sickness rates (people do not look for reasons not to go to work)
- Higher ratings in employee satisfaction surveys.

Better 'business performance' has been shown through:

- Higher standards of product or service quality measures (*effectiveness*)
- Higher output and better resource utilization (*efficiency*).

But none of this happens on its own, it has to be encouraged and supported. You cannot make people want to work in teams, to cooperate with each other or take on responsibility for their team's work, they have to choose to do it. Leadership is all about selling people your vision of how things could be, encouraging them to see the benefits for themselves and to work through some of the problems they will encounter. In particular, you have got to be prepared to let go, allow the team to take on responsibility and support their decisions, even when they make mistakes – only stepping in when the mistakes are likely to be serious. As we have already seen, leadership is about sharing power not holding on to it, and you have to allow the team to have some of your power, recognizing that this increases the total amount of power and does not take it away from you. Effective teams are only possible when there is effective leadership. If you cannot provide that leadership, the teams that you lead will never be fully effective.

Summary

- Group working has been around in various forms for nearly three centuries, since the beginnings of industrialization in the mid-18th century. It is based on the economic benefits of division of labour, which allow tasks to be broken down into their component parts and for specialized and large-scale equipment to be used.

- The increasing emphasis on group working was led by the Japanese 'quality' revolution in the period after World War II, and means that workgroups were expected to take on responsibilities that had until then been managers'.

- Group dynamics describes the internal working of groups and emphasizes the importance of the relationships and interaction between group members in ensuring the group's effectiveness. Tuckman's stages in group formation help to explain how these interactions and relationships develop as the group members get to know and understand each other, and work out how to work together.

- Under the right conditions and with the practical support of the organization, workgroups can become teams, if the members have a clear sense of direction, are committed to the team's goals and have worked out how to cooperate to undertake complex tasks, using the abilities of all team members.

- For teamworking to be effective, leaders must be prepared to work actively to encourage the teams by agreeing goals, helping rather than organizing, supporting team members' development, providing the right resources, removing any barriers to team-working, communicating effectively with all the team members and agreeing individual goals that support the achievement of the team's goals.

Notes

1 Taylor argued that there were four rules of scientific management:

First. They (i.e. managers) develop a science for each element of a man's work, which replaces the old rule-of-thumb method.
Second. They scientifically select and then train, teach, and develop the workman, whereas in the past he chose his own work and trained himself as best he could.
Third. They heartily cooperate with the men so as to insure all of the work is being done in accordance with the principles of the science which has been developed.
Fourth. There is an almost equal division of the work and the responsibility between the management and the workmen. The management take over all work for which they are better fitted than the workmen, while in the past almost all of the work and the greater part of the responsibility were thrown upon the men.
From The Principles of Scientific Management by Frederick W. Taylor (1911)

2 Bruce Tuckman first published his model (with four stages) in 1965 in an article called *Developmental sequences in small groups* (*Psychological Bulletin*, 63, 384–399). He added a fifth stage to the model 12 years later in an article co-written with Mary Ann Jensen, *Stages of small group development revisited* (*Group and Organizational Studies*, 2, 419–427).

9 Handling conflict

Conflict between group or team members is one of the biggest challenges faced by leaders, partly because it is so disruptive to the workplace, reduces performance and diverts attention from the achievement of goals, but also because it is hard for leaders to deal with. It is hard because it is, thankfully, fairly rare in most workplaces so leaders do not get a lot of practice in handling it, and also because it is something that can have significant implications for relationships between group members and between individuals and the leader. It is also the case that leaders are often judged by those they lead on the basis of their ability to deal with conflict successfully. Success or failure in doing so can spill over into all other aspects of the leadership role, especially into the level of trust that people have in you.

In this chapter we will look at some of the causes of conflict, at its effect on the work roles of everyone involved in the conflict, and at some of the strategies that you can use to deal with it. What is most important is to address conflict early on and be both firm in the way you handle it and consistent in your decisions. Handling conflict is probably the biggest test of your character, your communication skills, your personal integrity and your self-confidence. In the next few pages we will look at how you can do it effectively every time.

Conflict and its causes

Conflict can take many forms, ranging from mild disagreements to out-and-out physical violence. It includes:

- Disagreements or differences of opinion
- Complaints or criticisms of someone's performance, behaviour or attitude
- Excluding or ignoring others, or being disdainful or 'silently contemptuous'

159

- A matching of wills, test of power or threat to someone's control
- Deliberately acting in opposition to a request or instruction
- Perceptions that someone is being deliberately provocative or denigrating others' beliefs or rights
- Someone taking unnecessary risks or threatening the security of others
- Aggressive behaviour, yelling at another or being threatening.

Reflection

Have you experienced any of these conflict states?

- How well were they resolved?
- What role did you play in resolving them and how effective was the resolution?
- What did you feel afterwards? Did the resolution lead to a healthier work environment or did the problem continue to fester below the surface?

The nature of conflict

Conflict can flare up and die away in minutes or simmer for ages. The diagram in Figure 9.1 shows how different types of conflict are experienced along these two dimensions. Assessing these different types of conflicts, for their strength and the length of time they have occurred, is important in working out how best to deal with them, as we will see.

Generally speaking, conflict disrupts the workplace, makes it difficult for people to work effectively and creates a lot of 'negative vibes' – people feel psychologically upset by the conflict, even if they were not directly involved. How dysfunctional it is depends, in part, on its nature. On the whole, longer lasting conflict, whether strong or weak, is more damaging, but strong conflict is always likely to have a significant impact. However, this is not always dysfunctional, whereas longer lasting conflicts nearly always are.

There are occasions when conflict can be helpful in the process of identifying underlying problems (the conflict is the result of the

	Strong	
Short	*More significant outbursts and disagreements that flare up and are over quickly but may have long lasting effects, especially if they include violence or threats of it*	*Major disputes that may start weak but grow and lead to regular arguments or obstructive or threatening behaviour* **Long**
	Mild disagreements, differences of opinion or outbursts of frustration at others that are over quickly	*Longer-term dissatisfaction with the attitudes or behaviour of others can lead to low level feuding and disruption of work*
	Weak	

The vertical axis shows the strength of disagreement,
the horizontal axis shows the length of time it lasts

Figure 9.1   The nature of conflict

problem, not the problem) or in helping to generate new ideas. Sometimes, by bringing things into the open through argument it becomes possible to create stronger, more effective workgroups and teams. In particular, it prevents the low level grumbling that can make the workplace unhealthy and reduce individuals' performance.

In the rest of this chapter we will consider all types of conflict, from the mildest that is over in minutes to the most disruptive conflict that is very heated and long-lasting. In the process we will see how important it is to identify the nature of the conflict (its strength and length) and its causes before working out the best way to deal with it.

What causes conflict?

The most widely assumed reason for conflict is when people with different personalities clash. We have looked quite a bit at personality in *Introduction to Leadership* because it is critical in understanding how different people behave, and because it tends to be fixed ('hard wired') into people. However, it is useful to distinguish between personality and behaviour when looking at conflict. It is not personality itself that causes conflict so much as the differences in behaviour of people with different personalities (Figure 9.2).

Figure 9.2 Personality, behaviour and conflict

It is important to stress that personality might be fixed, but behaviour is a matter of choice (even if the choices are limited or difficult). That is why people with different personalities can work together quite effectively for many years, whereas others, with equally different personalities find themselves in conflict. What is it that makes people choose to behave in certain ways, ways that lead to conflict? The reasons are many but they include:

- *Emotional states* – these may not be connected to the issue over which there is conflict, but could be due to quite unrelated issues, not necessarily at work but at home or in some other area of activity. If someone is feeling anxious, upset, angry, worried, or some other emotion, conflict can arise through something quite trivial that just tips them over the edge. Such conflicts are likely to be short-lived unless the person's emotional state persists.

- *Conflicting opinions, beliefs or values* – when two people believe in something different, whether it is the existence of God or the rightness of some course of action, it can lead to conflict, especially if the belief or value is central to their life.

- *Power and control* – if people feel that their power or authority is being diminished, or that they are losing control over aspects of their work or the work of others, then this can lead them into conflict with those they see as taking their power and control. Power and control are often key features of people's perception of who they are and enhance their self-esteem. Taking this away is an attack on who they are.

- *Varying facts or data* – when two people have obtained different information about the same event or have used their knowledge to arrive at different conclusions then this can lead to serious arguments.

- *Alternative methods or processes* – if there are two or more ways of doing something, people can frequently get into conflict over which is better. This is frequently the result of new methods being introduced that are different from traditional ways of doing things and which can seem to some to be inferior or less effective. This can sometimes be due to people fearing their old skills are no longer as valuable when they have not acquired new skills.

- *Alternative goals* – when individuals or groups have conflicting goals, this can all too often lead to conflict between them. One of the reasons for you actively agreeing goals with the people you lead, as individuals and as groups or teams, is to ensure that their goals are in harmony. However, this may not help if people you deal with outside the group have different goals, or if people's personal goals conflict.

Before you can resolve conflict, you need to be able to identify what is causing it, not the least because some causes can be resolved far more easily than others. The steps you can take to resolve conflict all start from this initial question – what is causing this conflict to occur?

Resolving conflict

As a leader you must take conflict seriously – you will not be able to lead people anywhere if they disagree, do not get on, argue or are fighting each other. What marks effective leaders from the ineffective is that they are not prepared to stand back and allow conflict to occur when it can be avoided, nor will they pretend that it does not exist when clearly it does. Most importantly of all, leaders are able to resolve conflicts in which they are participants, the hardest part of all conflict management.

Thomas Jordan, a Research Fellow of the Department of Human and Economic Geography in Gothenburg, in Sweden, suggests these seven guidelines to help deal with conflict, guidelines which have been adapted here to provide a useful guide for a leader involved in conflict, in any circumstances:

1 *Ask yourself what it is you do not know yet*
   Keep in mind that you do not know what has happened before, especially in people's minds, and what they think is important and why. Start off by finding out what is going on, from everybody's perspective. Ask open-ended questions to help you understand the background to the conflict, including people's perceptions of what is significant in shaping their actions. You should also be open to learning new things about yourself and

how other people perceive you. Maybe others feel that you have contributed more to the problem than you are aware of.

2 *Make a distinction between the problem and the person*
Try to express the conflict issues as shared problems that have to be solved together. Avoid blaming people or giving negative opinions about others, but be willing to say what you feel and want and encourage the others involved to do the same. Distinguish between facts (what happened, how many times, etc.) and opinions, motivations, feelings and attitudes, and try to reach agreement on the facts of the situation first of all. People may not be able to agree on their opinions, but are more likely to be able to do so with the facts.

3 *Be clear, straightforward and concrete in your communication*
State clearly what you have seen, heard and experienced that influenced your views in the matter at hand, and encourage others to do the same. Conflict often stems from misunderstandings about what people meant. Get everyone involved to say what is important to them, why it is important, what they feel and what they are hoping for.

4 *Maintain contact between the parties*
Contact between the parties to a conflict is critical to resolving it. If people will not talk to each other they will not be able to resolve the situation. Work to improve relationships even if there are conflict issues that seem impossible to resolve. Encourage people to do something small that meets the wishes of another and suggest small things the other can do in return. However marginal they may be, these acts can help to change the nature of the relationship in a positive direction.

5 *Look for the needs and interests that lie behind concrete positions*
Find out what really matters to the participants in the conflict, so that if you cannot find the best possible solution, you establish the least worst for all parties, their absolutely minimum requirements to resolve the problem. Show understanding for people's feelings without letting yourself be provoked by their words or their behaviour, and encourage everyone to do the same.

6 *Make it easy for the parties to be constructive*
Do not allow people to start blaming, accusing or criticizing the other person or people involved. Show respect for everyone involved and ask them to do the same, no matter what they feel. Show that you care about the issues and needs that are

important to everyone involved, but demand that people take responsibility for their own contributions to the conflict.

7 *Develop your ability to look at the conflict from the outside*
Review the conflict history in its entirety. Notice what kinds of actions had positive and negative influences and think how you can influence the further course of events in the conflict in a constructive way. Accept responsibility for what happens and be prepared to take on problems as early as possible, before they have a chance to develop into major conflicts.

These seven guidelines depend upon exactly the same skills and characteristics we looked at in Chapters 2, 3 and 4 – having a clear set of values, being able to listen and communicate well with others, being honest and showing integrity in all you do.

Conflict management styles – between other people

People tend to approach conflict resolution in different ways.

Reflection

Do you recognize the three different styles listed below?

- Have you experienced them or have you used them yourself?
- How did you feel when the style was being used?
- Do you recognize the different ego states?

- *Accommodators* want simply to see an end to the present conflict and look for the easiest way to minimize its current impact by trying to accommodate everyone's point of view, needs and goals. They avoid making any judgements themselves about the rightness of different positions and focus on the effects of conflict rather than the causes. Their motto is *'let's all be friends'*; their policy is to take responsibility for the conflict rather than get those really responsible to do so.

- *'Stern parents'* attempt to stamp on the problem, treating all the parties as if they are naughty children who need punishing. Again they emphasize the effects rather than the causes and believe that they can use their power and authority to stop it happening. Their motto is *'do what I tell you'*; their policy is to blame everyone involved.

165

- *Mediators* look to find ways to resolve the problem so that it does not recur. They focus on the real causes and look for solutions that are acceptable to everyone. Their motto is *'treat the causes not the symptoms'*; their policy is to encourage people to take responsibility for their own actions.

Key idea

Transactional Analysis

Transactional Analysis (or TA) was developed by Dr Eric Berne as a way of describing how people relate to each other. He believed that we could each occupy three different 'ego states' (ways of thinking and behaving) that he called Adult, Parent and Child. The Adult state involves objective assessment and rational analysis, the Parental state is directive and judgemental, and the Child state is driven by emotional responses fixed early in our lives.

TA focuses on the way that social transactions (how we interact with other people) are based on certain combinations of ego state. Some are Adult:Adult (both parties are being objective and rational), some are Parent:Child ('I know better than you, so do what I tell you' – many leaders and the people they lead adopt these states), and so on. It is possible for each of the parties to any transaction to adopt one of the three states, producing nine possible combinations.

This is a very simplified way of explaining a complex idea, but Berne's model helps to make sense of the three main approaches to conflict resolution. *Accommodators* are essentially adopting a Child state and appealing to others to do the same – let us all kiss and make up. *'Stern parents'* are looking for a Parent:Child transaction in which the various parties do what they tell them and 'Stop being silly'! *Mediators* are asking everyone to be Adults and look at the problems objectively and rationally. This is not easy, because most conflicts involve people adopting a Child state and they have to be helped out of that state. Simply appealing to common sense does not work quickly because conflict often means that common sense has been suppressed by anger, fear, and other emotions.

Conflict management styles – when you are involved

Resolving conflicts between other people is hard enough, resolving them when you are involved yourself is doubly hard. The guidelines above are even more significant as you have to be as objective as you possibly can, and maintain an Adult ego state, even if everyone else is adopting the Child state.

Two questions you should ask yourself before attempting to resolve a conflict you are involved in yourself are:

- How important is it to maintain relationships with the others involved?

- How important is it to achieve a set of goals that are being hindered by this conflict?

In attempting to resolve the conflict you may well have to accept that one or other of these elements (relationships and goal-achievement) will suffer. Which is more important, not just immediately but in the longer term? Figure 9.3 suggests five possible strategies you can pursue:

Important

Winning matters
You know you are right, it is urgent or important to win and the other must give in to achieve the goals. This may mean you have to accept that a relationship will be damaged as a result

Work it out!
It really matters to get this sorted, because both the outcome and the relationship are very important. Why not ask a trusted third party to act as mediator to help you both achieve a resolution that you are both happy with?

Give a little, take a little
You both need to compromise but you can afford to give up some of what you want in order to preserve the relationship as well as you can

Goals

Ignore it
The issue is not important and nor is the relationship, so why make a fuss? Just ignore the problem and get on with what matters

Give in
It is far more important to maintain the relationship than it is to achieve a desired outcome, perhaps keeping a customer or supplier happy, or ensuring the team works well together

Unimportant   **Relationships**   *Important*

Figure 9.3   Conflict management – goals and relationships

- *Winning matters*, when the goal dominates and the relationship can be allowed to suffer

- *Ignore it*, when you can afford to let it go

- *Give a little, take a little*, when you both need to compromise

- *Give in*, when you really need to protect the relationship and can afford to lose out on the goal

- *Work it out*, when the goal and the relationship matter to you both.

Using your leadership ability

One of the biggest challenges for leaders is to balance their own needs and goals with those of the people they lead. This is what Robert Greenleaf meant when he talked about *servant-leadership*, the ability to put other people's needs and goals above your own when necessary. Conflict is not a pleasant experience, and there are times when it is easy to ignore other people's behaviour and hope that it does not happen again. Unfortunately, leaders cannot afford to turn a blind eye because they have a responsibility to those they lead to deal with problems for them. You should always put the welfare of those you lead before your own if you are to earn and retain their respect. In return you can expect loyalty and trust.

When conflict appears, meet it head on. Do not allow problems to fester or low-key conflict to run on until everyone gets used to tolerating it. Deal with it early and resolve it. If the problem is so severe that it needs to be treated as a disciplinary matter, treat it as one. But do not make threats if you have no intention of following them through. Equally, only use your positional power to push through a resolution when that is absolutely necessary (the matter is urgent or there is too great a risk if it is not resolved). The more important the issue, the greater the need for a resolution that everyone can accept, if that is at all possible. Do not try to pass on the problem to someone else, unless they are able to resolve it better – in particular, do not dump it on them because you do not want to deal with the conflict yourself.

Resolving conflict means:

- Being clear in your own mind about your ethical standards and values – what is right and what is wrong – and being prepared to stand by those in any discussion and decision.

- Recognizing how different personality traits affect how people perceive the world and their relationships with others, and accept that this is how they are.

- Being aware of your own and others' attitudes and motivations and the effect they have on their behaviour. Again, recognize that these exist and are important to people and cannot be ignored, ridiculed or changed easily by rational debate.

- Being emotionally aware, of your own and others' emotional states (be *emotionally intelligent*) and recognizing how they are shaping your and their behaviour. Emotions are much more amenable to change through discussion, although it may take time.

- Listening actively to what people are saying, reflect back to confirm and reframe if you can, to move them on to a more positive position.

- Using your ability to think through problems and work out the best solution, and being able to learn from past decisions to improve the effectiveness of your conflict resolution skills.

- Understanding the organization's goals and values and seeing how a particular conflict needs to be dealt with in the light of these.

- Seeing how individuals' personalities, attitudes and abilities have shaped their behaviour and what contribution development activities may apply in preventing future conflicts from arising.

In other words, conflict resolution draws on much of what we have looked at so far in *Introducing Leadership*, because it is a critical part of the leadership role.

Summary

- Conflict takes many forms and has many causes. Before you can start trying to resolve it, you must understand the nature of conflict, particularly how strong it is and how long it has been going on, and the causes of the particular conflict you are faced with.

- Before trying to resolve a conflict, think about the seven guidelines to make sure you address it effectively. Collect information, distinguish between the person and the problem, communicate clearly and effectively, keep the parties in contact, explore the underlying drivers of conflict, make it easy for all involved to find a resolution, and be objective and accept responsibility for the resolution of the conflict.

- Think about your 'ego state' when working to resolve a conflict and aim to adopt an Adult:Adult mediation style rather than being accommodating (Child:Child) or a stern parent (Parent:Child).

- When you are involved in the conflict, assess how important it is for you to maintain relationships with those you are in conflict with, and how important it is to achieve your goals. Look for a solution that reflects these two aspects, and do not be afraid to seek mediation help if you need it.

- Remember that conflict resolution is a critical part of being a leader and real test of your abilities. Effective leaders do not shirk this responsibility because it will reflect badly on the way that their followers view them, and reduce their effectiveness in their role.

10   Leadership in a crisis

It is much easier to lead people when everything is going well, when systems are working, people are performing effectively and you are making good progress towards your goals. It is when things go wrong that the real test of leadership begins, and the hardest test of all is when things go disastrously wrong. In this chapter we will look at the role of leaders in crises – in emergencies, during major stoppages and when all the goals get changed. We will start by looking at what we mean by a crisis and what it means to the people you lead, to the organization and to you as a leader. We will then go on to explore the role of leaders in crises and what knowledge and skills you need to perform the role effectively. Finally, we will consider what you can learn from crises, to prevent them recurring and to manage them better in future.

What is a crisis?

Most organizations operate in long periods of relative stability, with everything going more or less as planned or expected, and then, just occasionally, something goes wrong. But do not confuse being very busy or hectic with instability; being busy is a sign that the workload is high, maybe uneven, it is not in crisis. There are a few organizations that spend most of their time living on the edge, with enormous uncertainty, frequent unexpected events and constant changes of direction. The result is that what counts as a crisis for the majority of organizations would be regarded as business as usual for them. In other words, what people perceive as a crisis depends very much on what they are used to and expect, what the normal state is like.

For *Introducing Leadership* the words crisis, emergency and disaster will be used to mean something special, but how they are applied in different organizations may differ.

171

- A *crisis* is a situation that places severe pressure on people, that involves people doing unplanned or unexpected things and possibly having to perform tasks that they do not usually undertake, or having to do so under unusual conditions.
- An *emergency* is a critical incident that happens suddenly, without warning, and that may cause severe but short-term disruption.
- A *disaster* is a severe critical incident that may have built up over time or may happen suddenly, which is likely to have significant and long-lasting effects.

These definitions emphasize two main dimensions:

- the *severity* of the event and
- the *timescale* over which it occurs.

It is important to realize that crises may have different degrees of severity and may occur over very different time periods. A very severe crisis may suddenly occur, have an enormous impact for a short while but things then get back to normal very quickly. For example, a customer may cancel a major order or a production run may prove to have a significant fault. This can disrupt plans severely but once a new customer is secured or the production problem is overcome, the organization returns to normal and the crisis is put behind it.

Conversely, the problem may have long-lasting effects; the customer is not replaced, the organization has to make major redundancies and it starts on a long decline that leads to eventual closure, or the production fault leads to a large number of product recalls that cost so much money that an expansion programme has to be cancelled.

Emergencies, generally more severe crises that occur suddenly, include:

- accidents that cause injuries and deaths at work and/or that lead to major equipment malfunctions
- fires and explosions, lightning strikes, flooding, bomb scares
- computer systems or power failures
- criminal actions, including serious violence towards staff and robberies.

Many of these crises could prove to be disastrous if they were to cause major disruption to the organization's operations or even lead to its failure. But it is important to note that something that causes major but temporary disruption (e.g. a total systems failure) may have very limited long-term impact, whereas an attempted armed robbery may fail to have any serious impact on the organization at the time, but may lead to long-term problems because people working there feel anxious or unsafe and seek work elsewhere, leading to problems in maintaining output and adding to the organization's costs because of the need to recruit and train new people.

In other words, the severity of the crisis does not determine how long-lasting the effects may be; less severe events may last much longer and have a bigger impact, it depends so much on how the organization responds, which means how effectively it is led through the crisis. There are also lessons to be learnt from assessing the crisis to prevent it recurring or to ensure that the effects are reduced in future. That is why you should look at any crisis and ask yourself:

- How much warning did we have that this was going to happen? This includes signals that were overlooked or ignored, but are now clear.

- How severe is the impact now? Not how long will it last but what will the total impact be (output or customers lost, staff injured, jobs lost or people encouraged to look for work elsewhere, extra costs incurred or revenue lost)?

- Is it possible for the crisis to be overcome quickly or will it take some time, not just in recovering from the initial impact but any long-term effects. (Will it have a long 'tail'?)

What causes crises?

Many crises are unforeseen (and either unforeseeable or highly improbable) events that originate outside the organization as a result of circumstances over which the organization has little or no influence. Good examples of this are terrorist incidents, when a bomber targets a group of people almost at random because of where they are at a particular time. It was impossible for people working in the World Trade Center in New York in September 2001 or travelling to work in Madrid in March 2004 or London in July 2005, or for the people employing them, to foresee that the bombings would happen.

It was equally impossible for the people living or visiting beach areas around the Indian Ocean to foresee the Boxing Day tsunami which killed so many people so tragically, but the flooding of New Orleans or the earthquakes in Kobi and Pakistan were more foreseeable, even if their actual timing was impossible to predict. Therefore, we can say that some crises are caused by external events that could be foreseen (even if the actual timing could not be), making it possible to take action to reduce their impact (local flood defences, having water-sensitive equipment on upper floors, using earthquake-proof buildings, etc.) as well as planning for dealing with them, whereas others are not foreseeable and it is only possible to have general plans for dealing with the effects that a crisis of any kind might cause.

Crises caused by external events over which the organization may have some effect or control include crises caused by customers or supplier behaviour, or the behaviour of competitors. It is important to recognize that your organization may have more effect over the behaviour of others than you realize, if only because the effect is through what you do not do rather than what you do. Not caring about customers enough, not making your requirements clear enough to suppliers, not paying attention to your competitor's behaviour can all lead to unforeseen but quite predictable crises occurring.

Finally, there are crises caused by the organization's own actions or inactions. Not taking appropriate safety precautions or recognizing hazards at work, not making sure that employees are well managed or that equipment is well maintained can all lead to critical incidents. In 2005, a little while before *Introducing Leadership* was written, two major crises occurred which were both attributable to action or inaction by organizations:

- An oil storage depot near Hitchin, Hertfordshire caught fire and led to the destruction of the depot and its 60 million gallons of oil, and the evacuation of some 2000 local people.
- A strike by employees of Gate Gourmet, suppliers of food to British Airways, led to very negative publicity for both organizations and severe reductions in the quality of service for BA's passengers.

While each event may have been directly caused by something that was done (or not done), the true causes were far more systemic – the way that safety procedures were designed or enforced in the one case, or working practices and conditions of employment in the other. They are systemic because they arise from the way that systems are designed and operated in the organizations concerned. They may be unpredicted, but that does not make them unpredictable, nor does being predictable make them avoidable – you can see the crash about to happen and can do little to avoid it because the opportunity to do so has passed. All that is left is to minimize the damage the crisis does.

These different causes of crises are summarized in Figure 10.1 and should help you to focus on what could be done to prepare for all of them.

Category 1	External factors that are largely unforeseeable, over which the organization can take no action to control or influence them, or to minimize their impact
Category 2	External factors that are to some extent foreseeable, over which the organization can take no action to control or influence them, but can minimize their impact
Category 3	External factors that are to a greater or lesser extent foreseeable, which the organization can take action to control or influence and can minimize their impact
Category 4	Internal factors that are to a greater or lesser extent foreseeable, which the organization can take action to control or influence and can minimize their impact

Figure 10.1   The causes of crises

Preparing to deal with crises involves making *risk assessments*, judgements about the likely critical incidents that could occur, their severity and timescale, and the chance that they may occur.

- *Category 1* events may not be foreseeable and are very unlikely to happen, but their effect could be severe and even lead to the organization's failure, so the risk is very small but could be catastrophic. Although the July 2005 bombings in London or the 2004 Boxing Day tsunami were almost certainly unforeseeable (for any of the people and organizations affected), that does not mean that organizations cannot have generic plans to deal with events that have such a catastrophic impact, whatever their cause.

- *Category 2* events can and should be foreseen, even if they are very unlikely to occur, their possibility exists and the likely impact should be considered and taken account of in planning.

Where the cost of actions to minimize the impact is small and the actions are unlikely to have a significant negative impact, then why not take them, so that the impact is minimized, however slight the chance of anything happening?

- *Category 3* events are foreseeable, although they may be unlikely, and action can be taken to reduce the chance of them happening further. It is also useful to have plans for what to do if they do occur, plans that can be developed in more detail if the likelihood of something happening increases.

- *Category 4* events should always be foreseen and, ideally, the likelihood of them happening reduced as far as possible. If they appear likely to happen then plans for dealing with them should be prepared.

It is useful to distinguish between crises that it is possible to envisage happening, however unlikely they are, and those which are not, and to recognize that the possible outcomes are very much the same in either case. Just because you do not know what events might cause the organization to lose its buildings or a significant number of staff, does not prevent you from envisaging it happening and planning for the possible effects. This kind of *contingency planning* (planning for something that is contingent or depends on something else happening) is good management practice; it also demands effective leadership for the plans to be implemented.

Reflection

Have you ever experienced any of these critical incidents?

- Which category were they?
- How well prepared was the organization?
- Did any plans work?
- Do any plans for dealing with crises currently exist in your organization?
- Are all the different risk factors identified above recognized and planned for?

Again, at the time of writing, the possibility of an avian 'flu epidemic exists. The first outbreaks were in the Far East, but recent cases have occurred in Turkey, believed to be caused by migrating birds infecting domestic fowl from which it can be passed onto humans. What can organizations do to stop the spread of the disease? Unless they are involved in poultry rearing, not a lot, but they can plan for the effects of an epidemic of bird 'flu or any other, similar, event that could cause key staff to become seriously ill and lead to restrictions on movement of people domestically or internationally. How would the organization cope? Has it identified resources and systems it could use to cope with the situation temporarily? What would your role be in such a crisis?

The role of the leader in crisis

Risk assessments and contingency planning are good management practice, but effective leadership is essential if those plans are to be put into practice. Why? Because crises cause people to panic and lose direction (*headless chicken* syndrome), require decisive action with only partial or uncertain information, and involve people in working harder and better than they may normally have to do or do things that they may have little or no experience in doing. These all demand high standards of leadership to minimize the effects of the crisis and ensure people's safety and security, so let us look at each one to find out why they occur and what you need to do to deal with them.

Headless chicken syndrome

Most people like order and certainty in their lives. This is quite normal; disorder and uncertainty are stressful. Few people can cope with long periods of uncertainty, because it makes it impossible to plan or know what is expected of you. Crises mean that the normal order and certainty of the workplace have been disrupted, and people feel that they have lost control of their own world. The result of this is anxiety which can become panic if the crisis is particularly severe and/or sudden in its impact. This is when people start to behave like headless chickens – they cannot see what they should be doing or do not seem able to make sensible decisions. They have a tendency to assume that, since normality has disappeared, the normal rules no longer apply and lose any sense of direction, heading off in different directions because they do not know which way they should be heading.

What should an effective leader do? The first thing, in the immortal words of Corporal Jones (in *Dad's Army*), is 'Don't panic'! You should always stop and think about what needs to be done, taking as long as you can before arriving at decisions.

A crisis is not a time to forget what good leaders do in normal times, but to keep more closely to them. Many leaders become more directive or autocratic during crises; the best leaders consult and discuss their actions, to draw on the knowledge and skills of those they lead, but just do so more urgently. The only reason not to do so is in an emergency when there is a risk of serious harm if immediate action is not taken, and the right action is obvious. In other words, what is good leadership practice is still good practice, but more so, in a crisis.

Take decisive action with only partial or uncertain information

This is the most challenging aspect of leadership in crises – the quantity and quality of information is seriously reduced because the situation is unusual and the timescales get shortened. This is when true leadership comes to the fore, having to make decisions when you really do not know what is happening. The challenge for managers is that people look to them for leadership, especially when they feel anxious and uncertain. They are looking for leadership to provide certainty and reduce their anxiety and will judge you quickly by how well you provide that leadership. That means judging you by how well you decide on the actions that need to be taken.

In most non-critical situations you will make every effort to get the fullest information you can before making decisions. In crisis situations you may not have time to obtain as much information as you would like, or the information may not be available or reliable, yet you still have to make decisions. What you need to remember is that no decision is almost always worse than making the wrong decision, so:

1 Collect any available information to assess the situation to find out:

- what is happening?
- what has caused it?
- what are the immediate implications for you and the people you lead?

- what are the possible options for action?
- what plans have been made for this sort of situation?
- what is your responsibility?

2 Consult as widely as time and opportunity allows to:
- decide which option seems the most appropriate
- tell people what you have decided with confidence
- allocate tasks and actions, with a focus on using the skills and the abilities of those you lead
- eliminate or control the cause of the crisis
- limit the effects of the crisis on people, the physical environment, the organization and its operations (in that order)

3 Monitor closely what is happening

4 Keep your decisions under review and do not be afraid to change it if circumstances have clearly changed or more or better information becomes available

5 Report to the responsible person as soon as possible, to describe what you have learned and any actions you have taken.

How does this differ from decision-making when there is no crisis? In principle there is no difference – good decision-making should always follow more or less the same five steps, the only difference in a crisis is that the time for making the decision is condensed, so:

- You do not fully understand what is happening
- You do not have time to explore all options
- You are limited in whom you can consult
- Your assessment must be done quickly.

The pressure on time and the limited information available is not a reason for changing your approach to leadership and not consult people, which is the most common behaviour when leaders are under pressure. Too many leaders believe that they must make decisions on their own, because they believe this will demonstrate their decisiveness. Unfortunately, it is more about panic. The best leaders take time to make sure they have a proper understanding of the situation, no matter how slight, and are aware of the main options facing them. They do this by asking people simple but direct questions and listening carefully to what they say. They state the options that they can see, invite others to suggest any alternatives and comment on the choices facing them, before choosing what to do.

In a crisis, people can achieve more than they realize

Be decisive, say what you have decided and briefly say why, but do not debate the decision with people – it is too late now to consider the options again – but monitor the effects and be prepared to change your decision if it appears clear that an alternative would be better – but only if it is clear. Do not jump from one choice to another, willy-nilly. You must give people confidence in your decision, and that is most easily done by having confidence in it yourself. People are capable of achieving high standards of performance in crises if they believe that what they are doing is the right thing. You can help them to do this by inspiring that belief in them.

However, in crises, the tasks that people normally undertake may no longer be appropriate and they may have to do things that they do not normally do. Clearly, you should not ask (or allow) people to do things that are dangerous, but they may have to do things for which they have only limited knowledge or skills. To be successful they need the confidence to stretch themselves beyond what they are normally capable of doing, a confidence that you can help to provide by showing that you believe they are capable of doing it.

Learning from crises

In crises people, equipment, systems and procedures are all put to the test, and they do not always work as you would expect. Some do much better, others much worse. You should always make time to review what happened after a crisis and use this to learn and improve. The sorts of questions you should ask include:

1   Why did the crisis happen?
    - Was it something we, or others, did or did not do?
    - Should we have seen it was likely to happen sooner than we did?
    - If so, was there any action we could have taken, or anything we did that we should not have done?
    - Was there anything in particular that I should have seen, done or not done?

2 Did we react in the right way once the crisis emerged?

- Did we react fast enough, or too fast?

- Was there any information available that we could have used, but did not?

- Was any information we used shown afterwards to be wrong or misleading?

- Was there anything else we could have done that would have been better?

- Was there anything we considered doing that, with hindsight, would have been worse?

3 How did we perform in the crisis?

- Did people perform as well as expected?

- Did some people prove to be better or more effective than expected, or have skills we did not realize?

- Did any equipment fail or not perform as well as expected?

- Did any equipment designed to be used in a crisis prove to be unnecessary?

- Were our plans, roles and responsibilities for dealing with a crisis adequate and appropriate?

- Should any plans, roles and responsibilities be changed or created?

- Faced with the same situation now, would you make the same decisions and do the things the same as you did?

4 How did you perform, as a leader?

- Did you keep your head, follow any contingency plans and perform the role expected of you?

- Did you behave as calmly as possible, show confidence, and make decisions that were as well informed as possible?

- Did you inspire confidence in others, involve them in decision-making as far as you could, and keep them informed?

- What do other people think of your performance in the crisis? (How do you know? Have you asked them?)

Leadership in a crisis is a true measure of your leadership in normal times. If people trust and respect you, have confidence in you and are prepared to follow you normally, they will do so in a crisis.

Crises are not periods for unveiling leadership but for continuing to demonstrate it. If people are not willing to follow at other times, they will not do so in a crisis.

Summary

- A crisis is a situation that places severe pressure on people to do unplanned or unexpected things or perform tasks that they do not usually undertake, often under unusual conditions. It becomes an emergency if it happens suddenly, without warning, and a disaster if it has significant and long-lasting effects.

- Some crises are unforeseen and some are unforeseeable, but most can be prepared for, even if the likely causes are difficult to foresee. The worst crises are preventable ones, those that are the direct result of action or inaction on the part of the organization.

- A leader's role in a crisis is to keep calm and try to stop others from panicking, mainly by keeping to the rules of good leadership at other times, consulting and listening to others, making clear decisions and explaining them to people, but to do so in circumstances where there is less time or information than normal. That way people are given confidence that things are under control and the leader should be followed.

- Always review a crisis as soon as possible after it is over, to learn from it and make sure that, in future, the chances of it recurring are reduced but, if it does recur, that it is dealt with better.

11 Leading improvement

Most organizations these days claim to be committed to quality, to continuous improvement and to excellence. Unfortunately, far too many appear to believe that *saying* they are committed is the same as *being* committed. The reality is that not enough organizations really do ensure that goods and services consistently meet quality standards, that problems are dealt with promptly and standards raised, and that the organization excels in what it does (because that is what 'excellence' means). One major reason for this is that the organization does not have adequate systems and procedures, that people are not well enough trained and, crucially, first line and middle managers are not able to lead people effectively through the improvement process.

In this chapter we will look at what quality, continuous improvement and excellence mean, what needs to be done to make them a reality, and what your role is in leading people towards the achievement of the highest possible quality standards. In the process we will explore some of the history of quality management, continuous improvement and the search for excellence. One critical feature of this is the emphasis on shifting responsibility for quality to the people directly involved in the production of goods and services, along with the power to make the changes needed to fulfil this responsibility.

We all know what quality is, don't we?

If you have ever been on a course on quality, or read a book about it, you will know that they often start by asking what we mean by quality. If you are thinking, 'Oh not again!', do not despair, you will not be asked for your definition. Quality is what you or any other customer or user thinks it is, pure and simple. Any product or service you use is supposed to meet your particular need, and that is what we mean by quality, how well a product or service meets the requirements of its customers or users. This concept of quality, sometimes referred to as 'fitness for purpose', emphasizes that quality is subjective, it is what individuals think that matters.

This approach to quality, what customers or users require, contrasts with quality being products or services being produced 'to specification'. This view dominated manufacturing industry from its earliest days, setting out to produce goods for which there was a demand, but to do so to standards that were defined by those who designed the product, not the customers or users for whom it was being designed.

Key idea

Customers

Most managers and leaders do not need to be told that they serve both external and internal customers. However, the idea of describing users of some services as 'customers' is often unpopular with staff working in the provider organizations and among the supposed customers of those organizations. Medical staff have patients, schools and colleges have pupils and students, social services have clients and service users, railways have passengers, and there is little evidence that patients, pupils, students, clients, service users or passengers want to be called customers – what they want is to be treated like customers, to be treated as if their requirements mattered.

It is useful to distinguish between labels and ideas. Calling people customers does not mean that their requirements are treated as paramount; treating people as customers means exactly that – their requirements are what drive the organization. Throughout *Introducing Leadership* we will use the word 'customer' to mean the people who are the buyers or users of products or services. This means it includes:

- the people who buy and consume products or services (and often one person in the family buys but the family as a whole consumes)
- the people who use public services that are paid for either by taxation or by service charges
- organizations which purchase goods and services, and their employees who use them

- other people in an organization who depend on the products and services produced by colleagues in the organization (internal customers).

However, the word customer is an idea and does not have to be used as a label for the people who buy or use the products or services, and the best organizations recognize the difference.

The idea of quality as products and services being what designers meant them to be like sounds reasonable, but leads to problems. The worldwide growth of the Japanese motor industry in the 1960s and 1970s was based on giving customers what they wanted, not what car designers thought they should want. The competition between Betamax and VHS in video recording and between 8 track cartridges and audio cassettes was won by the technically inferior products that more closely met customers' requirements. Given the choice between cars with radios as standard or that were charged for as extras, or the chance to buy electronic goods that offered more choice of recorded films or were smaller and more flexible, customers went for what engineers thought were technically inferior products because these products did what customers wanted.

More importantly, products and services that meet customers' requirements must do so consistently, because consistency means that customers know that they will get what the organization says they will get. What is often labelled the 'Japanese quality revolution' that took place from the 1950s onwards (in Japan) and that was slowly introduced in Europe and North America in the late 1970s, was based on these two ideas:

- Quality is defined as what customers require not what designers think they should have
- Products and services need to be produced consistently to a standard that meets customer requirements.

What really matters is continuous improvement

Consistency does not mean no variation, only that the variation is within the acceptable limits. Any variation that occurs within these acceptable limits is due to random fluctuations, because people and equipment will never be able to repeat every operation exactly the same. This random variation is sometimes called *special cause* variation (the name given it by W Edwards Deming, one of the great 'quality gurus') because each example is due to something special which can often be difficult to predict or control. This can be as simple as a person feeling tired or a hot day causing machines to change slightly. When processes go out of control or there is a consistent pattern of faults, this is called *common cause* variation (because of a problem each sample has in common).

This distinction is important because Deming argued very strongly that the people operating the process – on a production line, in a call centre, on a hospital ward, or wherever – could do something about special cause problems, because they were often responsible, but only managers could do something about common cause problems. This is because they are due to design faults in the process and only managers could change these. However, the people operating the process are best able to identify the causes and ways of doing something about them. Managers should involve people in monitoring their processes (not inspectors), so that they see problems as soon as they occur and do something about them. Managers should help them by making sure they have the skills to:

- do the job properly
- monitor their own work
- identify the causes of problems
- find solutions.

In particular, managers should lead them through the process. What is now often called Total Quality Management (TQM) or continuous improvement or *kaizen* (a Japanese word meaning 'good change') relies on effective leadership of workgroups and teams. Remember leadership is *the ability to bring about movement or change in a group or organization, when there is risk or uncertainty, by inspiring others to head in a particular direction.* Continuous improvement is based on the idea that constant, small, *incremental* (in small steps) improvements are often better than occasional large-scale improvements. Coping with the constant change and uncertainty implied by that, inspiring people to take responsibility for improvement and ensuring that the changes being made are in the right direction, all need effective leadership. This is helped by remembering a simple process invented in the 1930s by the quality pioneer Walter Shewhart, and popularized by Deming, called the 'Shewhart cycle' but usually remembered as *PDCA* (Figure 11.1).

- **Plan** what you are going to do to improve the process
- **Do** what you have planned
- **Check** that it is producing the desired results
- Put the change into **Action**

Figure 11.1 The Shewhart cycle

This idea is that you do not simply decide what to do and then go and do it, but plan what to do by involving everyone likely to be affected, try it out and then check to see if it is working. Only then do you put it into action, making appropriate changes if they are needed. Effective leaders have the skills to discuss possible changes with others, and are not afraid to try things out and change them if they need changing. Poor leaders hide their lack of skills by not involving others in decisions and then, having made decisions, are afraid to change them.

Everyone is committed to improvement, aren't they?

One of the biggest problems with ideas like 'quality', 'TQM', 'continuous improvement' and '*kaizen*' is that nobody is going to say that they are against any of them, but they often fail to learn what they really mean in practice. When Walter Shewhart first developed his approach some 70 years ago, it meant challenging the scientific management approach that Frederick Taylor had advocated and which had revolutionized manufacturing. Taylor removed as much responsibility as possible from the people involved in processes, whereas Shewhart wanted to increase it. Although some of Shewhart's methods were used in the armaments industry during World War II, it was not until they were taken from there to Japan in the 1950s (by Deming and fellow US engineer Joseph Juran) that they started to become widely used.

The basic ideas are simple:

- Quality means designing and producing products and services that meet customer requirements rather than what producers think they should want

- Key aspects of processes need to be monitored to ensure that the process is under control

- Processes are in control when there are only random variations due to special causes, when people and equipment are working as they are expected to work

- Processes are out of control when there are common cause problems (such as poor training or recruitment, or wrongly specified or maintained equipment)

- Those closest to the process are best able to monitor what is happening and identify what needs to be done to rectify problems, using the PDCA cycle to guide them.

Unfortunately, too many managers misunderstand or feel threatened by these ideas. Misunderstandings include believing that every new product or service has to be thoroughly tested by asking customers if they want it. The trouble is that the most innovative products come from someone having a good idea and seeing if they can sell it. The best example is the Internet, something that has grown exponentially in size and use without people ever knowing what it could do for them until they explored it. There is also a tendency for organizations to measure those aspects of a process that can be measured, rather than those aspects that really matter to customers. Targets are set without discussion and far too many resources are put into measurement, too few into improvement.

David Mead, who was Chief Operating Officer at Internet bank *First Direct*, an organization that regularly gets rated as one of the best service providers in the UK, criticized other call centre operators in 2000 for their emphasis on call duration – the shorter the better. First Direct was far more concerned with ensuring that the people dealing with customers discover what customers want and then do not just meet those requirements but exceed them. This contrast between keeping calls short (meeting the organization's requirements to keep costs low) and not just meeting, but exceeding, customers' requirements shows the importance of measuring what really matters for customers. Mead also described how First Direct employees had monthly meetings with their team leaders to discuss their performance, with the focus on coaching to help improve that performance.

In late 2005, the Consumers' Association magazine published a survey of the public's views on retailers. Two of the top three places were occupied by the John Lewis Partnership and its food retailing arm, Waitrose. What people valued was the combination of service provided by the stores and the value of the products they supplied – not their cheapness. This ability to meet or surpass customer requirements is what helps an organization stand out from its competitors, and it is the front line customer facing staff who make the difference for most people. That is why the people who lead them are so critical to the organization's success. If they do not share the passion for quality and the ability to inspire the people they lead to share that passion, then customers will not experience the quality that they want.

Using standards

Standards are the way that successful organizations meet (and surpass) customer requirements. What are standards? Standards are the measures by which an organization judges its products, its services and itself. They are the way that organizations translate what customers require into words and measures that reflect what the organization does (its processes). For example, Tesco has recognized that its customers hate waiting in queues at checkouts, so it has promised that, if it can, it will open more checkouts. Of course, the key words are 'if it can'. If all checkouts are operational or there are no more staff available, then there is not a lot it can do. However, it is possible to count the length of queues periodically and record these data – if more than three customers are waiting and:

- there are some checkouts not open and staff are available, then there is a special cause problem
- all checkouts are open, then there is a common cause problem.

If it is a special cause problem then the people working in the store are able to solve it but they cannot solve a common cause problem, it needs capital investment. As a first line or middle manager you need to be able to distinguish between these two types of problem in meeting standards and recognize your leadership responsibility in either case is to:

- ensure that the special cause problem is resolved as quickly as possible
- push those managers responsible for doing so to resolve a common cause problem.

But you should also ask 'Is this the right standard?' Do customers really care about having to wait in the queue, and is the standard (three people and we will try to open another checkout) appropriate? It may well be that what customers really want is not having to queue at all, and the three people rule is the nearest any store can afford to achieve if it is to be price competitive. This is the problem facing organizations – to set standards that are as close as possible to what customers require but are also feasible and achievable – that are economical and practical. Set standards low and they are more likely to be achieved and customers to be dissatisfied; set them too high and they are less likely to be achieved and customers will still be dissatisfied. The best standards satisfy or, better still, delight customers and are achievable (and stretch the people trying to achieve them).

Standards may be called targets, especially if they are quantitative, such as sales achieved, reject rates, bed-nights, success rates, etc. However, when the standards relate to aspects of customers' experience, as First Direct believe, targets for the time the call takes can actually reduce the quality of service. Instead, standards should emphasize less easily measured but far more important characteristics. Effective leadership means that these standards are not less valued because they cannot easily be measured, but are treated seriously because you show through your own behaviour that they matter. This might be a focus on establishing good relationships with customers or being alert to minor faults that customers may not even see. Furthermore, by focusing on how well people perform, through observation and discussion, and by helping people to improve, by giving feedback, coaching and training them, you can ensure that standards are met and raised over time. That is continuous improvement.

Leading improvement

It is one thing to know that a process is not under control; it is another to be able to do something about it. Leading groups of people to improve a process is a key role for any first line or middle manager who is committed to continuous quality improvement. There are several ways of approaching this but, generally speaking, there are two main ways of working; one involves working with the workgroup or team who are responsible for a process, the other with a group of people who get together to make improvements to aspects of the organization's operations that cut across individual workgroups or teams. These are sometimes called quality improvement teams or quality circles, and normally consist of people who have volunteered to work on the improvement.

In either case, the improvement process usually involves six stages:

1 Agreeing and clarifying the problem – what is it that needs improving?

2 Collecting and analysing information about the problem – how big is it, how often does it occur, what does it cost, etc.?

3 Identifying the root cause of the problem – what really causes it to happen?

4 What constraints are there on resolving it – what are you allowed to do, what are you not able to do (e.g. 'any improvement must pay for itself within one year')?

5 What options are available to resolve the problem? – this is sometimes called 'opening up', to explore all possible options available

6 Which option is most likely to resolve the problem best, within the constraints that exist ('closing down')?

Having got agreement to the improvement, if you need to, you would then move onto the PDCA cycle, planning the implementation, doing it, checking and putting it into action. Let us look at each of these six stages in a bit more detail.

1 Agreeing and clarifying the problem – what is it that needs improving?

Being clear about the problem and agreeing what it is may seem minor, but can be surprisingly contentious. You may be concerned about an increase in customer complaints, but the customer service team may be concerned about increasing customer threats. They think the problem is that they are too exposed and want a panic button and a glass partition between them and customers, whereas you think that the problem may stem from how they are treated before they reach the team. The purpose of the exercise is to find out what is causing the problem but, if you cannot agree on the problem, you will not be able to find out its cause. So, define the problem clearly and as objectively as possible, trying to avoid saying what has caused it. In this example, the problem could be 'An increase in the number and intensity of complaints'.

2   Collecting and analysing information about the problem

This is a critical step; how big is the problem, what are the effects (waste, lost customers, repair, etc.), how often does it occur and what does it cost, etc.? Understanding the costs of quality is important because poor quality and high quality both cost money; the trick is to spend money on ensuring high quality and not on putting poor quality right. There are three types of cost of quality:

- *Failure costs* – These are all the costs associated with failure to conform to or perform to requirements, including the costs of lost market share due to customers' perceptions of quality

- *Inspection or appraisal costs* – These are the costs incurred in inspecting, monitoring and testing for conformance to requirements in products or services

- *Prevention costs* – These are the costs of all the activities needed to prevent problems occurring.

Joseph Juran (one of the early pioneers of quality management) argued that the pattern of these costs changes as organizations become more committed to continuous quality improvement (Figure 11.2).

Initially, the Failure costs account for the bulk of quality-related costs, as organizations fail to deliver the products and services customers require, so they get thrown away, reworked, returned and replaced, customers fail to return and money has to be spent on attracting replacements. The first step in overcoming these problems is to step up the Inspection or appraisal effort, and resources

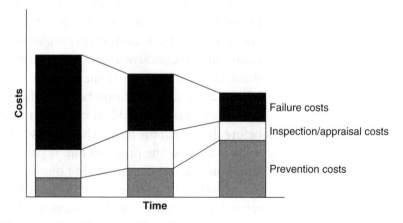

Figure 11.2   The costs of quality

are used to check items, monitor service delivery and generally impose tight controls on what is done. Only when the third stage is reached, when the organizations build in systems and procedures to ensure that problems are identified and resolved, are those problems prevented and quality standards achieved and raised. The process is one of gradually shifting the costs from 'Failure' to 'Inspection' and then to 'Prevention', reducing the total cost of the process. The ideal goal is *zero defects*, when problems are eliminated or reduced to a level that makes the cost of further improvement so great as not to be worthwhile.

As well as considering the costs of quality when deciding whether or not action needs to be taken, it is useful to have a clear picture of the scale of a problem. The easiest way to collect data on a problem is a simple *check* or *tally chart*. This involves recording a problem each time it occurs, using a simple gate count. This is one of Kaoru Ishikawa's 'Seven tools and techniques of quality improvement' (Figure 11.3). Ishikawa was one of the first major Japanese quality improvement figures, following in the footsteps of Deming and Juran. He emphasized the importance of the people in workgroups and teams collecting and analysing data on quality themselves, and used simple tally charts to show that it was not important to have complex systems, just accurate ones.

Having collected the raw data, they need to be analysed. Scatter charts, bar charts or histograms can help to see patterns easily and quickly, and convince people that something needs to be done. As a leader committed to quality improvement, you must make sure that everyone shares your desire to do something. By showing them the scale of the problem clearly (which charts do much better than tables of data), you can convince them of the need to do something.

A Pareto chart is slightly more complicated, but can demonstrate the scale of a problem very well. It is based on the principle that there may be a whole range of different quality problems but a few of them account for the majority of the failures to meet customer requirements, what Juran named the 'vital few', as opposed to the 'trivial many'. (By the way, Pareto was an Italian engineer turned economist who identified that the majority of a nation's income was received by a small minority of people, giving his name to what is sometimes called the 80:20 rule.) The bars in the chart show the number of problems accounted for by each type, in descending order of occurrence. For example, an Internet and mail order

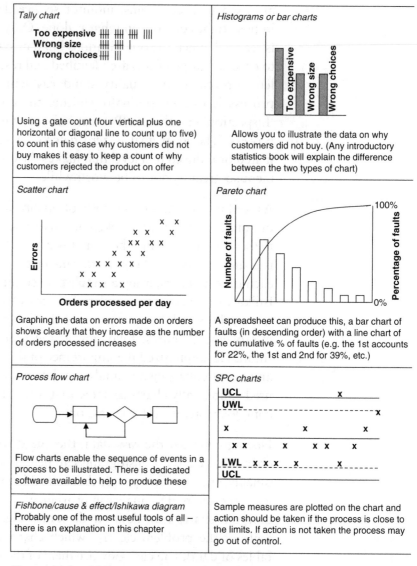

Tally chart	Histograms or bar charts
Too expensive ⦀⦀ ⦀⦀ ⦀⦀ ⦀⦀ ‖‖‖‖ **Wrong size** ⦀⦀ ⦀⦀ ‖ **Wrong choices** ⦀⦀ ‖‖‖	
Using a gate count (four vertical plus one horizontal or diagonal line to count up to five) to count in this case why customers did not buy makes it easy to keep a count of why customers rejected the product on offer	Allows you to illustrate the data on why customers did not buy. (Any introductory statistics book will explain the difference between the two types of chart)
Scatter chart	*Pareto chart*
Graphing the data on errors made on orders shows clearly that they increase as the number of orders processed increases	A spreadsheet can produce this, a bar chart of faults (in descending order) with a line chart of the cumulative % of faults (e.g. the 1st accounts for 22%, the 1st and 2nd for 39%, etc.)
Process flow chart	*SPC charts*
Flow charts enable the sequence of events in a process to be illustrated. There is dedicated software available to help to produce these	
Fishbone/cause & effect/Ishikawa diagram Probably one of the most useful tools of all – there is an explanation in this chapter	Sample measures are plotted on the chart and action should be taken if the process is close to the limits. If action is not taken the process may go out of control.

Figure 11.3   Ishikawa's seven tools and techniques of quality improvement

company may analyse customer returns over a one-month period and find that the reasons are as shown in Figure 11.4.

In this example, the first two reasons for returns account for 61.8 per cent of all returns; the first three account for 77.8 per cent – these figures appear in the third column and simply result from progressively adding up the percentage figures in the middle column. The conclusion from this? By doing something about the

Reason (in descending order of importance)	No:	%	Cumulative %
Item not what was expected/required	62	38.3	38.3
Wrong size or colour	38	23.5	61.8
Damaged in transit	26	16.0	77.8
Arrived too late	17	10.5	88.3
Ordered wrong item (entered wrong code on order)	12	7.4	95.7
Changed mind	7	4.3	100.0
Total	162	100	

Figure 11.4 Reasons for customer returns

first three problems, 78 per cent of returns will be prevented. Better descriptions and information on the website and catalogues and improved packaging are most likely to resolve the problems.

3 Identifying the root cause of the problem – what really causes it to happen?

Resolving problems properly means understanding their causes. Leadership helps to do this, because leaders are able to ask probing questions and are not satisfied with easy or comforting answers – they prefer the truth, however unpalatable it might be. In fact, they are not satisfied until they have uncovered the root cause of the problem. The root cause is the real, underlying problem. For example, problems with equipment may well be put down to equipment failure then, after checking, to poor operation. However, this is in turn due to poor training, which is due to the people doing the training not having had any training in how to train! So the root cause is the lack of training for trainers, and until that is solved the equipment problems will not be fully resolved. More importantly, other problems may also be resolved which have the same root cause.

The tool which is best at helping to identify root causes is the *fishbone* (named because of how it looks), *cause and effect* (because of what it does) or *Ishikawa diagram* (because of who invented it). Fortunately, these are different names for the same thing. The fishbone diagram (the easiest name to remember) looks a bit like a fish skeleton, with a spine and four main bones radiating out, two above and two below. The 'spine' should have an arrowhead on its right end pointing to a box; the four 'bones' radiating off should be labelled:

1 *People* (their roles, relationships, number, skills, training and performance)

2 *Resources* (facilities, equipment, tools, machinery and materials used)

3 *Monitoring* (inspection, checking, data collection and analysis of performance)

4 *Processes* (what tasks people do, how they fit together and how they operate).

The problem to be solved is written in the box that the 'spine' points to, as this is what is being solved and the causes all lead to. A brainstorm session (see Chapter 12 for details of how to lead one of these) will help you to identify the likely causes or factors leading to the problem and these can be sorted into the four types (People, Resources, Monitoring or Processes) and then entered onto their 'bone'. Where one factor is seen to cause another (e.g. poor training leads to poor operation of equipment), this is shown as a smaller 'bone' leading off the main 'bone'. This is illustrated in Figure 11.5.

A whiteboard can be useful in putting together your fishbone chart, with the people working on the problem gathered round and collaborating on creating it. Good leadership means involving others

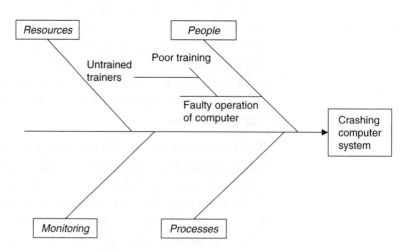

Figure 11.5   A fishbone diagram

and encouraging them to take part in deciding on the causes and their effects, and not trying to do everything yourself.

4 What constraints are there on resolving the problem?

Before starting on the problem-solving process you need to find out what you are allowed to do and what you cannot do. These are the constraints you are working under, and they may limit the resources you can use, the payback period (how quickly any solution must pay for itself in savings made), or any health and safety concerns you must take account of. Effective leaders are open about constraints, because they would otherwise mislead people as to what is possible and what is not. Where you think that constraints are unrealistic, do not be afraid to tell this to the people who have set them, but once they have been agreed you must 'sell' them to the people you are working with to solve the problem.

5 What options are available to resolve the problem?

In Chapter 12 you will learn about innovation and creativity, which involves people thinking of ideas without any constraints, sometimes called 'opening up', to explore all the possible options.

6 Which option is most likely to resolve the problem best?

Again, in Chapter 12 you will get the chance to explore the 'closing down' process in more detail, filtering ideas until they become feasible.

Leading excellent performance

Leading improvement is not easy, just critical to the success of any organization. As people have become more and more demanding, the organizations that supply products and services have had to respond to their expectations. In a society where people can contact suppliers every hour of the day and every day of the week, where next day delivery has become the norm and where loyalty to suppliers lasts only as long as the next transaction, organizations cannot afford to relax. This is as true in the public and voluntary sectors as it is in the private sector. Hospitals and schools, local councils and Government agencies are all expected to be more sensitive to the requirements of their 'customers'. Clubs, charities, trades unions, building societies and associations are all expected to operate to the standards that people experience elsewhere.

Leading improvement is the key to ensuring that what your organization does meets these demanding requirements. You may not be involved in identifying customer requirements directly (although if you deal directly with customers you can be alert to what they say and do, to help identify them), but you should always be asking yourself how well what you and the people you lead are doing meets or exceeds them.

Increasingly, organizations have found that being able to meet customer requirements is just not enough. Too many other organizations can do that. Products are more reliable, services are available instantly, prices have fallen in real terms, often delivering better quality at lower prices. The best example is the personal computer, something that has fallen in price almost as fast as its power has increased; the ability to access information and entertainment from around the world, communicate with people next door or on distant continents as easily as logging on and launching a simple piece of software has become so common that we easily forget that this has all happened in less than two decades.

This is why organizations have to look beyond what people require to what they had not realized they could experience, to delight them with the excellence of what is available. Excellence means exceeding expectations, consistently. It means adding value to products and services in ways that customers did not anticipate, but which solves problems or meets needs they did not know they had. It is important to distinguish between this and simply 'tarting up' your products or services to make them appear better, without adding any real value. Value is about real benefits to the customer or user. As a leader you should always be looking beyond what you currently do to seek out improvements that help your organization stand out from the crowd. In Chapter 12 you will learn what you can do to create a culture of creativity and innovation, which underpins excellence, but you need to start the process by:

- Never being satisfied with 'adequate' or 'good enough', always strive to exceed expectations, to be the best
- Ask yourself what would make customers recommend the organization to other people, and do it

- When things go wrong do what you can to put them right, and make sure it does not happen again
- Set yourself performance standards that stretch you but are achievable and then, once you have met them consistently, raise them.

Excellence is as much a state of mind as a set of skills or activities. It is the state of mind that effective leaders have, looking forward in the direction that they want to go and making sure that people follow them.

Summary

- Quality is about meeting customers' requirements, consistently. Excellence is about exceeding customers' expectations, so that they obtain greater value for money than they had expected.
- Ensuring quality means having clear standards and monitoring performance to see how well those standards are being met. Continuous improvement is about improving performance and raising standards over time, in small steps. The six-step process involves:

  1 Agreeing and clarifying the problem
  2 Collecting and analysing information about the problem
  3 Identifying the root cause of the problem
  4 Identifying the constraints on resolving the problem
  5 Exploring the options available to resolve the problem
  6 Selecting the option most likely to resolve the problem best.

- All leaders should be able to use the tools of quality improvement if they want to ensure that their organization really does meet customer requirements.

12   Leading innovation

Innovation – and creativity – are key elements of quality improvement and the search for excellence. People tend to assume that creativity is something that only a few people are capable of and so innovation is something only a few organizations can achieve. While it is true that some people do seem to be naturally more creative and that some organizations are consistently innovative in what they do, do not think that this means that most people and organizations just have to follow along behind, copying what the leaders do.

Most people are capable of being creative and most organizations can be innovative if they have the will and the leadership to be so. You can provide that leadership for the people you manage and can inspire them to be creative or, to be more precise, to release the creativity within them. In this chapter of *Introducing Leadership* we will look at what it means to be creative and how this relates to innovation, what leaders can do to encourage creativity and how that creativity can be channelled into developing innovative processes and delivering innovative products and services.

Understanding creativity and innovation

Dr William Coyne, the senior vice-president for research and development for the 3M Corporation[1], defined innovation and creativity as follows:

- *Creativity* is the thinking of novel and appropriate ideas
- *Innovation* is the successful implementation of those ideas within an organization.

In other words, creativity is the idea and innovation is putting those ideas into practice. Organizations need to encourage creativity if they want to be innovative, but creativity is not enough to ensure innovation – too many organizations have come up with really novel ideas but failed to exploit them effectively or the ideas just have not been appropriate, there just was not a market for them.

So let us explore these two concepts in turn and see how they work together.

Encouraging creativity

More or less everyone is capable of being creative, given the right opportunity and encouragement. You may well feel that you have met people who are so unoriginal in their thinking that they could never come up with a creative idea, but do not be fooled. What limits people's creativity is that they have not had the opportunity or the encouragement. But let us start by seeing what creativity is, and what it is not. Bill Coyne defined creativity as 'thinking of novel and appropriate ideas', which means that creativity can be found in a whole host of different settings.

We tend to think of artists and writers, poets and musicians as creative, but that is a very limited view. There are many artists who are creative, but the majority may be technically accomplished whose ideas are derivative, their painting and writing just pale imitations of original, creative works. On the other hand, when Newton discovered the laws of motion and Darwin discovered evolution, when Brunel designed the SS Great Western and Ortzon designed Sydney Opera House, they were being as creative as Michelangelo or Van Gogh – thinking novel and appropriate ideas. Creativity can be found in all walks of life and at all levels. It is found in the little things we do as much as the big things.

> *Reflection*
>
> - What do you think is the most creative idea you have ever come across, in art, literature, music, science, engineering, philosophy or the humanities?
> - What is it about your choice that really impresses you – its originality, its expression (i.e. what it is in practice), what the creator had to go through to make it happen, or what?
> - What is your own most creative idea or action? What can you look back on, with pride, and say, 'I did that'?

Unfortunately we learn early in life to judge how other people will react to our ideas, and we process all our thoughts through an internal 'filter' to assess whether or not they are likely to fit into what people normally expect. We avoid making outrageous suggestions or thinking really imaginatively; creativity involves by-passing those filters and letting our minds roam freely to come up with the unusual, untried and sometimes absurd ideas that form the basis of innovative processes, products and services. Creativity can help you to solve quality problems by looking for novel ideas that will become innovative solutions.

Creativity is particularly valuable in stages five and six in the quality improvement process, which is why we have left these two stages to this chapter. They are:

- What options are available to resolve the problem? (Stage 5)
- Which option is most likely to resolve the problem best? (Stage 6).

Your role, as a leader, is to encourage people to be creative by using some simple but effective techniques that just require a little bit of confidence on your part. Five of the most common of these are outlined below:

1 *Brainstorming.* This is probably the most commonly used technique for generating original ideas, and also the most abused (because people do not know how to do it properly). Your role in leading a brainstorming session is to encourage and even pressurize people to come up with as many ideas as possible, allowing plenty of time and accepting long periods of silence as people struggle to think up something new. One form of pressure is to insist on a fixed number of ideas, say 30 or 40, to encourage people to really go to extremes in their thoughts. There are a few, very simple principles, but they are frequently ignored:

- Focus on quantity rather than quality
- Postpone judgement – nobody may comment on anybody else's ideas and only ask questions to clarify what they mean (all too often people start discussing ideas too early)
- Build on each other's ideas but do not argue with them
- Freewheel, encouraging changes of direction.

2 *Charting unknowns.* This is a form of reverse brainstorming; rather than coming up with ideas for what you can do, you focus on what you do not know about a problem or a possible new way of working. Asking what you *do not* know is a good

start to investigating the issue and searching for information. Again, it encourages creativity by making people examine a problem from a variety of different angles.

3 *Nominal group technique*. This is a complex name for a fairly simple technique, similar to brainstorming but not as public. Instead of calling out ideas in a brainstorm, a group works individually, each person writing three ideas on a sheet of paper and then passing this on to the next person in the group, who adds three more ideas. The process is repeated until the lists are back where they started or nobody can add anything. Each person then reads out an idea from their list, in turn, with others chipping in with variants from their lists (which they can continue to add to as further ideas are stimulated). This encourages people who are shy (more introvert) to play an active part, and the different ideas act as triggers for further ideas.

4 *Metaphoric thinking*. Metaphors are ideas or things that are similar to the topic being explored or have similar qualities. For example, a company having problems with goods damaged in transit might look at other fragile goods that are packaged safely, like eggs in cartons. Transporting eggs become a metaphor for the company's transport problems. A similar approach involves using a dictionary, opening it at random and picking the first word on the page, then looking for links between that and the topic you are considering – it may sound daft, but it gets people's brains working in the most creative way.

5 *Lateral thinking*. This is an idea invented by Edward de Bono, and he has put forward a number of different ways of encouraging thinking that breaks away from convention. One is the *intermediate impossible*, developing the most outrageous solution possible (solve the damaged goods in transit problem by wrapping them all in thick cushion foam so that they bounce) and then work back to some intermediate position that will actually be viable.

There are plenty of books and websites with suggestions for techniques to use during creative problem-solving sessions, but the only way to find out how to use them is to try them out. It may seem a bit alarming at first to ask people to be as outrageous and off the wall as possible, but one feature of creative ideas generation is that it makes people laugh if they are really into it, so it should be fun and effective at the same time. Try doing brainstorming, charting unknowns or lateral thinking standing up around a whiteboard or flipchart, rather than sitting down, and you will find that people then become more involved and will often move around to be next to people whose ideas they really like, a useful way of identifying support for the suggestions being made. Keep groups sizes low but not too small, say around seven people, because that creates the right group 'dynamic' (sense of purpose and internal relationships), with five as a minimum and nine as a maximum.

From creativity to innovation

Creativity alone is not enough; as a leader your job is ensuring that creative ideas get translated into innovative action. Creativity involves getting people to open up to new ideas – what is called *divergence*. Divergent thinking is another way of talking about creativity, looking for ways of doing things which have never been thought of before because they turn received opinion upside down. Once the ideas have been generated you need to sort them and decide which ones are worth developing, which is called *assimilation*. You should not discard ideas that are too different just because they are off the wall; sort through them and find the bits that are worth using. This takes more time than developing the original ideas and is when the real breakthroughs can occur, when the impossible starts to be seen as the possible. Divergence and assimilation are the two main components of Stage 5 in the quality improvement process (*What options are available to resolve the problem?*) and are the creativity phase ('the thinking of novel and appropriate ideas').

It is worth having more ideas than can actually be used at this stage for the move onto the final stage, Stage 6 (*Which option is most likely to resolve the problem best?*). This involves *convergence* or closing down, deciding just what to go ahead with. As you learned in the last chapter, the criteria for deciding should have already been agreed, so the selection of the final choice(s) is based on rational decisions and not just what people feel most comfortable with. This leads on to *action*, to implementing the decision. Convergence and action are the translation of the creative ideas into new processes, products or services, the innovation phase (the successful implementation of creative ideas within an organization).

You should remember that innovation is often a threat to those for whom it may offer the most benefits. Other managers may feel threatened and the first steps in doing something truly innovative may be a bit messy, as you learn how to make it work effectively. Francis Bacon, the great philosopher, writing in 1625, said that: 'As the births of all living creatures are, at first, misshapen, so are all innovations…'. Your novel ideas will not necessarily translate into practice very easily, and this can be disheartening, but if innovation were easy, every organization would do it!

Many organizations are not well-disposed to innovation because they do not want these 'misshapen' processes, products and services messing up the well-organized world they are used to. You need to be prepared to sell your ideas, but this will be much easier if your organization welcomes creativity and innovation. Bill Coyne identified six characteristics of 3M that he believes have enabled the company to be innovatory, despite their size and age as a corporation (Figure 12.1).

Just to make sense of what these characteristics mean, in 1923 an R&D engineer at 3M, called Dick Drew, was researching abrasives used by garages when respraying cars (at a time when two-tone cars were becoming popular) and came up with the idea of

Vision	Not just a sense of purpose but a purpose which explicitly includes innovation and one which is constantly translated into practice by employees. *Vision* is where we want to go
Foresight	The ability to predict accurately where customers are going, not just where they are now. It involves identifying their needs, both the *articulated* need, reflecting problems that customers are aware of, and *unarticulated* needs, those requiring a real insight into what the customers really require
Stretch goals	People need to be pushed to go beyond simple incremental improvements. 3M's stretch goals include: • 30% of sales to be from products introduced in the last 4 years • 10% of sales to be from products introduced in the last year This creates a sense of *urgency*; innovation is time sensitive, missing opportunities can seriously harm the organization's future
Empowerment	This means more than empty rhetoric, it means giving people some say over how they use their time and make decisions about how they do their work
Communication	This means creating an open organization in which horizontal contact and networking is possible, enabling multi-disciplinary teams to be created and the cross-fertilization of ideas to occur
Rewards and recognition	Having reward programmes covering innovation, often based on peer recognition (rather than managers' judgements), promotion on a *dual ladder* to either advanced technical grades or to management posts, but not direct financial rewards for specific innovations – that is their job!

Figure 12.1   3M's approach to innovation

masking tape, a tape that could be peeled off and not damage the paint underneath. Decades later another 3M R&D person, Art Fry, found a use for an adhesive that did not stick properly when he invented Post-it™ notes. Both were able to do this because, at 3M, technical staff have the right to spend up to 15 per cent of their time on projects of their own choosing. This time is not measured, but is a notional concept which creates a climate in which individual initiative is positively expected! For every 1000 ideas, only 100 become formal proposals, and only a few of these become new product ventures – of which over half fail – yet without the climate of innovation the company would not be able to remain at the forefront of innovation in its many markets.

Reflection

- Does your organization encourage innovation? Is it open to creativity and suggestions for improvement that involve radical changes in processes, products or services?

- How well do you encourage creativity among the people you lead? Are you open to innovative suggestions for improvements?

What really stands out about the 3M approach is that the characteristics that Bill Coyne identified are much the same as those we have defined as being necessary for effective leadership – having vision and foresight, setting stretch goals, empowering people, communicating and rewarding and recognizing achievement. Effective leadership is an essential element of innovation, because without a sense of direction and the ability to change, innovation is pointless.

Leading innovation

The leaders of innovation workgroups and teams must attempt to be one step ahead of those they are leading through the creativity and innovation process. This establishes a goal-setting way of working because, as the leader, you should be thinking ahead and leading the group through the sequence of divergence, assimilation, convergence and action, helping them to be creative and come up with innovative ideas, not trying to come up with them yourself.

You can help divergence, the opening up of ideas, by:

- encouraging people to search for ideas, inside and outside the organization

- remembering that quantity breeds quality, so do not make judgements nor allow others to do so

- encourage a '*yes and*' rather than '*yes but*' mentality – good ideas get killed too quickly by finding reasons not to accept them ('Yes, but we can't....'); an innovation leader must encourage a 'can do' mentality, which means looking for ways round obstacles ('Yes, and we can ...').

Reflection

Think of a situation when someone has come up with an idea that has been met with the response 'Yes, but...' (or something similar). In other words, one or more people have immediately seen the downsides, the barriers and problems involved in doing what has been suggested. How did you feel? Was it your idea, or were you the person who said 'Yes, but...'?

Now consider how you might have said 'Yes, and...'. 'Yes, and...' means looking at the ways that any barriers can be overcome or any other benefits that might come from the idea, focusing on the positives not the negatives. In creative ideas generation, the purpose is to find ways of being innovative, not reasons not to.

Assimilation (sorting) and convergence (selection) can be done by:

- *clustering* – bringing together similar ideas to see how they compare or may be combined (3M's Post-it™ notes are useful here – write the ideas on individual notes and then move them around into groups)

- using *hurdles*, increasingly difficult constraints which the suggestions must pass over, filtering out those that do not cross the hurdles

- *ranking* the different ideas, giving each of them a score out of ten and putting them in rank order, or pair them up randomly (use Post-it™ notes again!) and move them up and down against each other until they are in order

- *weighting* – awarding points depending whether they have desired features or do not have undesired features (with a different number of points to reflect the relative importance of each feature)
- when all else fails, using *instinct* – what feels right.

Tudor Rickards[2] suggests that putting creative solutions to problems into action, being innovative, is helped by having:

- *open communications*, so that creative solutions do not seem to have arrived out of the blue; the process of innovation should not be cloaked in secrecy
- *reward systems* (but not necessarily financial ones) which encourage and recognize innovation – some organizations give originators of ideas a share in any savings or extra revenue generated
- *autonomy for individuals*, allowing people to find different ways of solving the same problems, fostering a diversity of views within the workgroup or team
- *senior managers as role models*, creating a climate in which innovation is welcomed, not resisting it.

Unfortunately, organizations can resist innovation because of dominant *mind-sets*, which create self-imposed barriers to change. A mind-set is simply a fixed set of ideas and ways of thinking that limit the options that are considered when looking at problems. People with fixed mind-sets often make unwarranted assumptions about the effectiveness of existing and new approaches – the old way is always better than anything new. They tend to adopt a 'one-correct answer' way of thinking and do not like any challenges to what is currently done ('it ain't broke so don't fix it') coupled with a very negative response to any new ideas ('we tried that once and it didn't work' or its converse 'not invented here' syndrome) and pressurize others to conform. Above all, they often have a fear of looking foolish by challenging what everyone accepts as normal or, even worse, trying something new and failing at it. As Tom Peters says (in *Thriving On Chaos*), the worst kind of organization is the one that does not make mistakes, because mistakes come from taking risks and long-term success is dependent on risk-taking, which sometimes does not work. All mistakes are a chance to learn, and the successful organization celebrates failure.

Leadership, innovation and risk

Organizations that resist innovation lack leadership. Leadership is about movement and change, it is about managed risk-taking (knowing what risks can be taken and which should be avoided), about having a vision and willingness to try new ideas to fulfil this vision. Unfortunately, all this involves stepping outside your comfort zone, moving away from the safety of what you know to the uncertainty and hazards of what you do not know. Leading innovation involves being able to assess risks and still move forward.

Most first line and middle managers are familiar with the hazards and risks associated with health and safety at work; the hazards and risks associated with innovation can be approached in the same way.

- Hazards are the potential for harm
- Risk is the probability of it happening.

When you look at any innovation you should ask the two questions:

1 What could go wrong (hazard)?
2 What is the chance of it happening (risk)?

But, as well as asking it about the innovation, you should also ask it about the current option – what is the risk of doing nothing? You can use a simple risk assessment method, the same as assessing health and safety risks (Figure 12.2). There are various ways of scoring harm and risk; in the example both are scored out of five, so the maximum combined measure is a score out of 25 (5×5). Both Option 1 and Option 3 present very low risk to the organization, whereas 'Do nothing' is as risky as Option 2. However, alongside the risks of harm are the chances of benefits, using the same rating scale. Option 3 (a relatively low risk option) also offers a

	Potential harm	Risk	Harm × Risk	Potential benefits	Chance	Benefit × Chance
Option 1	1	2	2	2	3	6
Option 2	4	3	12	5	3	15
Option 3	3	1	3	4	2	8
Option 4	5	4	20	3	2	6
Do nothing	4	3	12	1	4	4

Figure 12.2   Assessing the risk of innovation

210

INTRODUCING LEADERSHIP

good chance of some benefit, and Option 4 (the highest risk option) offers a similar potential for benefit. Some higher risk options (e.g. Option 2) may offer the chance of more substantial benefits, but this needs to be balanced against the risks.

The assessment of risk and potential benefits does not tell you what you should do, it simply spells out the risks and the benefits – leaders make decisions and the best leaders make the most informed decisions. Making a decision is all about making a judgement, information simply helps to compare the alternatives better. In practice, the scale of risk and benefit in the chart is less important than the discussion that takes place to agree the figures in the chart. The numbers give a spurious sense of something scientific being done when, in fact, the figures are themselves judgements based on experience and informed guesswork. What the chart does is to force you to consider both sides of the equation (risks and benefits) and to distinguish what might happen from the chance of it occurring.

All too often we get hypnotized by the hazards ('If this goes wrong we could be bankrupt!') rather than assessing the probability of it happening and what can be done to reduce that probability. If two trains or two planes hit each other the results are disastrous but it rarely happens because the precautions that are put in place are made as foolproof as possible. By comparison, cars crash every day, making it the highest risk option of the three, and the risks arise from the failure of drivers to follow standard safety measures. When you are considering creative ideas, look at the hazards of doing something innovative, but also look at the chance of something going wrong and what steps could be taken to minimize this risk. Pilot projects, small-scale trials and gradual introduction of innovation can all help reduce the risks and make it possible to get the benefits, which you should also assess in the same way.

Innovation and power

Innovation needs people who are willing to think creatively ('outside the box'), but it also needs the organizational culture that welcomes and encourages innovative ideas, and that means giving power to people to make innovation happen. This is because people are only able to innovate and change the way that things are done if they are allowed to make decisions, and decision-making is about having power. A first line or middle manager must either possess the power, or must be able to identify who has the power, to make things happen (and, also, who has the power to prevent it). This means finding out what the priorities of the people with power are and working with them, building alliances to show how the changes you want to introduce are in line with their goals; challenging someone's aims or values is not an effective way of building alliances.

According to Rosabeth Moss Kanter[3], organizational power depends on:

- *Information* (data, technical knowledge and expertise, political intelligence)
- *Resources* (money, materials, space, staff, time)
- *Support* (endorsement, backing, approval, legitimacy).

The first of these, *information*, means that leaders must know about the new processes, products or services that they are proposing to introduce. They should set out to be the authorities on the issue and what it means for it to be implemented in their own organization (including the risks and benefits of doing so). They need to work with the people they lead to seek knowledge and share it, encouraging different people to take responsibility for investigating particular areas and become the 'group expert', identifying sources, making contacts and undertaking reading. The sum of the individual expertise will be greater than the amount each individual could hope to develop in the time and with the resources available.

Whatever *resources* are needed, there will never be enough! Leaders must identify what resources there are available and make the fullest use of them and build alliances to share resources from other sources. They should not attempt to duplicate what is being done elsewhere in the organization, but look for ways of opening up access to get more out of resources. The time available must be used as effectively as possible by planning activities, allocating targets and reviewing progress on a regular basis, not getting side-tracked and allowing interesting activities to distract them from important ones (remember the *Urgent/Important* grid – see Chapter 4).

Support from above is crucial, from the *gatekeepers* and *sponsors* who can make things happen or put barriers in your way.

'Gatekeepers' are those people in power who can allow you to do things, or who can stop you from doing them. 'Sponsors' are people who may not be able to let you do things or stop you from doing them, but can provide support for your ideas with those who do have the power to say 'Yes' or 'No'. This is something successful salespeople are very aware of – the Finance Director (sponsor) may not decide on the purchase of new machinery, but without the Finance Director's support, the Production Director (gatekeeper) will not sign the order.

When you are planning how to introduce an innovation in your area (the *action* phase of innovation) you should think carefully about these three issues:

1 What information do I have and need?

   ● Who has the information?

   ● Who is best able to obtain any information that is needed – become the 'group expert'?

2 What resources do I need?

   ● What resources do I have access to?

   ● What other resources are available, and who controls access to them?

   ● Can I share resources or take advantage of what is happening elsewhere?

   ● How can I make best use of what is available?

3 What support do I need?

   ● Who are the gatekeepers who can decide whether or not the innovation is possible?

   ● Who are the sponsors whose support is crucial in bringing the gatekeepers on-side?

   ● What are the goals of both gatekeepers and sponsors, and how well does the innovation align with them?

Leadership is all about making things happen, and leading innovation is a real test of your abilities as a leader. The challenge is great but the benefits can be enormous. Increasingly, innovation is becoming the critical feature in determining the long-term survival of organizations. Your role is critical in making innovation happen, because you have responsibility for the people who operate innovative processes and provide innovative products and services to customers and users. You should embrace creative thinking and innovation and inspire those you lead to do so as well.

Summary

- Creativity is the thinking of novel and appropriate ideas; innovation is the successful implementation of those ideas within an organization.

- Everybody is capable of being creative; the role of leaders of workgroups and teams is to enable people to use their creative abilities to solve problems and improve the quality of processes, products and services.

- There are various techniques that leaders can use to enable creative ideas generation; there is no great mystique about them, it just requires confidence to try them out.

- The creative process means encouraging divergent thinking ('opening up') and assimilation (sorting and grouping ideas to find the one worth pursuing). Innovation is about putting those ideas into practice, through convergence ('closing down') to find the ideas that will really work and then putting those ideas into action.

- Innovation involves risk, and leaders need to be able to assess the hazards and risks of innovations, but also the benefits and the chance of gaining those benefits, so that an informed assessment and decision-making occurs, challenging fixed mind-sets that resist innovation.

- Information is not the only requirement for making innovation happen; action also requires resources and support, from gatekeepers and sponsors, to turn creative ideas into innovative processes, products and services.

Notes

1 Dr William (Bill) Coyne was delivering the sixth UK Innovation Lecture at the Queen Elizabeth II Conference Centre on the 5th March 1996. 3M's reputation for innovation is reflected in its being at the forefront of all the technologies in which it operates, a strategy that encourages and rewards creativity.

2 In his book *Stimulating Innovation: A systems approach* published by Palgrave Macmillan in 1985. Tudor Rickards has written widely on creativity and innovation; another useful book is *Creativity and Problem Solving at Work* (Gower: 1990).

3 In her excellent study of different organizations' ability to change, called *The Change Masters* (published by Allen & Unwin: 1983).

13   Leading change

In Chapter 11 we looked at the importance of leadership in quality improvement and in Chapter 12 at the need for leadership in ensuring that improvements are made by using the creativity of the people you lead to ensure that the organization can be innovative in its processes, products and services. In this final chapter we will focus on the need for leadership in enabling change to occur, not just the incremental changes that are central to quality improvement but the step changes that organizations have to make periodically, where every element of the way you work may be shaken up.

In the early 1990s, there was a period when many organizations were keen on 'business process re-engineering' or BPR, a name that was coined by two American authors[1]. Although their ideas were sound, the way that they were popularized and adopted was not, and many organizations made some serious mistakes in the fundamental changes they made to the way that they worked. In this chapter we will look at BPR and why it offers some sensible guidance on how to approach change. But before doing so, we will look at what the pressures are for change, and then, having explored BPR, what you need to be able to do to lead change successfully.

Why change?

In 1997, Diane Coyle, then economics editor of *The Independent* newspaper, wrote a book called *The Weightless World*[2]. In her Introduction to the book she makes the point that the people living in industrialized countries were 20 times better off at the end of the 20th century than they were at the beginning, in terms of their standard of living and general economic welfare, yet the total weight of goods being produced and consumed in those countries was no greater than it was 100 years before. The closure of steel mills across Europe in the last couple of decades has not been because we are driving fewer cars or making fewer journeys by train or car, quite the reverse, but the vehicles we travel in are made with far less steel. The radiograms that took up space in our grandparents' and great-grandparents' sitting rooms have been replaced by MP3 players and iPods, the half dozen or so 'phones that most families now have take up less space than the single telephone that was the most any household expected to have twenty years ago.

What Coyle describes is a fundamental change in the way that economies now operate. Goods are becoming smaller and their life cycle – the period from their invention to demise – is getting shorter. In 2005, Dixons, the electronic retailer, announced it was no longer selling video players because people were no longer buying them. Across the country, video stores have started to close down because people are not renting them any more. Instead, they are either buying DVDs or renting them, but not from retail outlets. Instead, they are using Internet-based rental companies, which generally operate on a subscription basis, and can offer a choice from 40 000 or more titles which are sent out by post. In 30 years, video stores have appeared, grown and started to disappear, but their replacements may last for even less time than video stores, because of the possibility of supplying 'content' as electronic downloads rather than supplying the physical product. The book-size video is replaced by a digital signal. No plastic needed for the physical product; no shops, lorries or people to distribute and store the product; no energy expended in collecting and returning the product. Just a website, a telephone line and a hard disk, all of which can be reused time and time again.

What about jobs? The original production cast is still employed, but the people who physically manufactured and distributed the product no longer have their jobs. Instead the website designer, Internet Service Provider and call centre employee (staffing the Helpdesk when the download does not work) have jobs. Unfortunately, they can be anywhere, and are as likely to be in Bangalore as in Birmingham or Bournemouth. This is globalization, the opening up of the world economy so that goods and services can move around the globe effortlessly and cheaply. The weightless world means that distance becomes less and less important. The huge cost of installing infrastructure (whether it's optical fibre lines to transmit digital signals[3] or a container ship able to carry 9000, 6 m (20 ft) containers[4]) means that the more that is carried, the lower the unit cost.

Leadership in a 'weightless world'

What has all this got to do with leadership and change? Because the rate of change in knowledge, in technology and in how we live our lives means that no part of the economy is immune from these developments. People have to live with greater levels of uncertainty, causing stress and making people feel that they can have no loyalty to their employer because their employer can no longer offer any guarantees to them. This uncertainty is not confined to the private sector either. Privatization, public–private partnerships, the private finance initiative, compulsory competitive tendering, best value, league tables and targets, are some of the very many policies that have hit the public sector and led to wholesale changes in the way people work and who they work for. The private and voluntary sectors are now major suppliers of services to the public on behalf of Government instead of Government doing the work itself, which means regular re-tendering and fixed term contracts for staff.

Leadership in this context has become more and more necessary because people feel that they live in a world without trust, and they need to feel trust to have confidence in the world about them. Leaders, as we know, have to be trusted to perform effectively and so leadership is one way that organizations can give people the stability that they look for.

To provide that leadership and earn that trust you need to be able to cope with the pressures of change and help people to respond positively to the changes that they experience. Change is not bad nor are people naturally afraid of it. What they fear is the uncertainty of change, the lack of control (that it is 'done to them' rather than something that they have some power over) and the feeling that they do not matter. To do this you need to understand what is causing the changes that affect you, the people you lead and your organization.

The pressures for change

Organizations exist in a world where changes are happening all the time. One way of trying to make sense of these pressures is a *PESTLE* analysis (Figure 13.1).

Each of these headings can be used to analyse the external environment within which the organization operates, identifying what

Political	Political pressures for change include decisions by local councils, national Governments, and supra-national bodies (the EU or the World Trade Organization). Different organizations are affected in different ways at these different levels of political decision-making. For example, small business may find its local council prevents it from expanding, national government imposes new rules on its operations and the WTO removes trade protection that brings in cheap imports.
Economic	Economic pressures for change include both the state of the national and international economies (including exchange rates) and the markets the organization operates in, including the competition it faces and the behaviour of customers. For example, a reduction in interest rates encourages people to increase their mortgages to pay for house extensions and improvements, or a competitor introduces a new product that cuts demand for your organization's products.
Social	Social pressures for change include changing demographic characteristics (an ageing population living and working longer), changing attitudes, expectations and behaviours. For example, there are now more older than younger people in the UK, affecting the demand for all kinds of goods and services, including health and social care.
Technological	Technological pressures for change are critical in many organizations, affecting how the organization produces goods and services, what goods and services it supplies, and what other goods and services customers may use that could affect the level of demand for what the organization supplies. For example, the development of mobile 'phones has significantly altered the way many people work, making them far more mobile as they can now access information anywhere and keep in touch permanently with their base.
Legal	Legal (or legislative) pressures for change can affect all aspects of an organization's activities, including the employment of people, design of processes, sale of goods and services, finance and governance, and information. Each change in the law can mean changes are needed in some aspect of the way the organization works, and some of these changes can have a knock-on effect, requiring further changes in related areas. For example, legislation to prohibit disability discrimination has led to many products being redesigned and retail outlets altered structurally, to avoid prosecution.
Environmental	Environmental (or ecological) pressures for change are of two forms – those that arise from the increasing concern internationally about the environment and the effect this has on the other areas listed above, to encourage more environmentally-friendly behaviour by organizations, and those that arise (or may potentially arise) from a changing physical environment and climate. For example, rising sea levels in parts of East Anglia are causing local councils to abandon attempts to prevent coastal flooding and allowing farm land to turn to salt marsh.

Figure 13.1   PESTLE analysis

pressures for change exist and the likely effect they will have. Of course, they also interact with each other – legal changes arise from political decisions, and can have social and economic effects. This analysis of the external environment, identifying pressures for change and their likely consequences for the organization, is not about certainty but probability – what *might* happen or what *might* be the effect if it does. Some pressures will be stronger than others, and some will have a greater impact on the organization than others.

- One of the challenges of *management* is to make judgements about what kind of changes are likely and what effect they are likely to have.

220

- One of the challenges of *leadership* is to make judgements about how people will respond to these changes, what effect it will have on them and how they can be encouraged to recognize any opportunities that may arise from the pressure to change.

Reflection

What are the main pressures for change on your organization? Use the PESTLE framework to assess these pressures and ask yourself these questions:

- How will the people you lead respond to these changes?
- What effect is the change likely to have on them? In particular, what opportunities does the change offer them?
- What do you need to do to encourage them to recognize any opportunities that may arise?

Many changes seem to have only negative effects for people – job losses, skill redundancy (their skills are no longer relevant) or less attractive working conditions. There is a limit to what any leader can do in helping people to seize opportunities when those opportunities are not worth seizing. Leadership means being honest and trustworthy, and effective leaders do not pretend that bad news is really good. What leaders can and should do is to be honest, telling people the truth and being as open as possible. The bad news is always worse than the fear of bad news, and the ability to manage decline is as much the mark of an effective leader, if not more so. This is where your ethical standards (Chapter 2), your character (Chapter 3) and your skills (Chapter 4) as a leader are tested, but if you know what your values are, if you have the strength of character and personal skills that you have been encouraged to develop by *Introducing Leadership*, then you will cope well with the challenge.

The ability to change

In Chapter 5, you were encouraged to undertake a personal SWOT to assess your own development needs. You should do the same for your organization and for your part of it; a SWOT analysis compares the external pressures for change with an analysis of the organization's capacity to respond and to determine its development needs. You will remember that SWOT stands for:

- Strengths
- Weaknesses
- Opportunities
- Threats

Strengths and *Weaknesses* are internal and all about the characteristics and features of the organization. They reflect the capacity of the organization to respond to external pressures for change, while *Opportunities* and *Threats* arise from what is happening outside in the external environment, the results of the PESTLE analysis. As a leader, the questions you should be asking about the internal abilities of the organization, its strengths and weaknesses, are:

- *How well are people prepared for new roles and responsibilities, in terms of skill levels, attitudes and commitment?*

  People who are well trained are usually more open to retraining and learning new skills than people with low skills or who have not taken part in training for some time.

- *How open is the organization, internally?*

  Is it easy for people to move from one area of activity to another, for workgroups and teams to be reformed and processes redesigned to cope with new patterns of demand and new operations? Is the organization flexible, with *permeable boundaries* between its different parts? ('Permeable boundaries' is a term used in systems theory and refers to the way that the organization is divided up into its different component parts, and the ease with which they deal with each other. An organization with permeable boundaries is one where people, information and resources can move easily around the organization.)

- *Does the organization have a culture that welcomes change rather than being afraid or resistant to it?*

  Culture has been defined as 'the way things are around here' and is hard to define but easy to identify in the language people use, the symbols and dominant mind-sets.

There are limits to what you can do to change the whole organization, its policies, culture, management strategies and leadership. However, you should make sure that the part of the organization that you lead is as ready for change as possible, taking advantage of every opportunity for training your people, being as open to other parts of the organization as you can, and encouraging a culture that welcomes change.

Business process re-engineering

Business process re-engineering (BPR) is a simple idea that can be devastating in practice. It starts from a completely different position than most approaches to change – they tend to ask:

- Where are we now?
- Where do we want to be?
- How do we get there?

This is often called 'gap analysis' because the focus is on the gap between the two positions. But its weakness is that you look at where you want to be from where you are – if you look out your front window at home what you see is what is across the road, because that is the perspective you are looking from. What you see is the difference between your own home (seen from inside) and the house opposite (seen from the outside). But stand out in the road and both houses may look exactly the same. Your perspective, the view from where you stand, determines how you see the rest of the world. It is the same with change; ask where you want to be and the perspective is from where you are, and that shapes your perception of what is possible.

A different perspective

BPR tries to change that perspective, by asking (as the CEO of Proctor and Gamble Inc said a few years ago):

If the organization did not exist today, how would we create it?

Most organizations grow and change organically, adding a bit here, chopping a bit there. The result is the organization as it exists is not designed for what it does but what it used to do, but updated. There is also a desire to keep the organizational structure simple, because this makes it easy to manage. The accountants are all in the finance department, the engineers in production, etc. Lines of control and accountability are clear and straightforward. On the

223

1. Several jobs are linked together in multi-disciplinary teams

2. Employees are involved in decision-making, usually working in teams responsible for the whole process

3. Processes are organized in the natural order – from materials in to finished goods out, or enquiries 'in' to completed insurance policies 'out'

4. Single processes have multiple versions, allowing for variation in what is produced, rather than separating out each variant into separate operational or production units

5. Employees work where it makes most sense, so accountants may be spread out through the organization, for example, overseeing all aspects of the financial aspects of a process or group of processes

6. Checks and controls are reduced to the key aspects, especially reconciliation between actual and 'book' volumes (with responsibility for accuracy lying with those who operate the processes)

7. Case managers provide a single point of contact for the whole process in a hybrid centralized/decentralized structure

Figure 13.2   The characteristics of re-engineered organizations

other hand, processes, the things the organization does, are complex. Goods are ordered by one department, used by another, paid for by a third, sold by a fourth and despatched to customers by a fifth. It is easy to show on an organization chart, but not on a process flow chart (which illustrates the process).

The people who buy materials and services never meet the customers that buy the products or service those materials and services are used to supply. BPR changes this by moving from simple organizations with complex processes to complex organizations with simple processes. Figure 13.2 shows what this means in practice.

Two simple case studies illustrate the way that re-engineered organizations work:

- An insurance company used to handle claims by having all claims logged on receipt by a clerk who passed them to claims administration where someone would process it and pass it to a loss adjuster to determine the value of the loss. From there it went back to administration who advised the client and, if the value of the loss was agreed, the claim would be paid, by passing it on to accounts. Claims would take months, with most of the time spent waiting between receipt, logging, loss adjusting, etc. The re-engineered process had teams of administrators, loss adjusters and accountants working together, with the whole case dealt with by the team. Claim times were reduced to around three weeks at most.

- A factory making plastic packaging for a toiletry company used to produce all its plastic mouldings in one department, print them in another and then despatch them in a third. Most of the time large quantities of semi-finished or finished goods were sitting in storage, waiting for the next process. Under the re-engineered system, raw material was fed into a cell (production area) through a large network of pipes and the mouldings came off the plastic moulding machine straight into the printer. Finished goods were packed up and taken straight to a loading bay, into a container that, once full, was despatched to the customer.

The principle behind BPR is to reduce the delays in the system to the minimum, build the organization around the processes and give responsibility for quality, delivery (of products or services) and management of the process to the teams operating it. Managers, instead of managing complex processes now have to lead complex organizations, a much more challenging but satisfying task, because customers' requirements (the definition of quality) become the driving force for the organization, not a bolt-on extra.

If you are trying to change the way that your part of the organization works, a full re-engineering change project is difficult, because re-engineering is an organization-level approach. However, you can still ask the question about your area of operation:

If it did not exist today, how would we create it?

This provides you with the chance to consider radical change to improve the processes, products and services you are responsible for.

Being a change leader

We saw in Chapter 12 how you can encourage people to be creative and develop innovative solutions to problems or ways of working and, in this chapter, how you can go about identifying the need for more profound change and how BPR can contribute a radical new perspective on what you do. But you still have to make change happen, and that is where your abilities as a leader are put to the test.

Styles of change management

All too often, when major change is being made to an organization, managers adopt one of two styles:

1 A *Rational-Empirical* style, which assumes that people are rational and will accept a logically argued case for change,

225

especially if there is some incentive for them to do so – simply explaining that this redesigned system works better than another will convince people to accept change.

2 A *Power-Coercive* style, which assumes that people will do what they are told. A new system is designed, based on a detailed analysis of what was there before, to remove any problems or respond to external pressures for change, and then people are told how they will now work. It uses the authority of managers and the ability to coerce people by using threats to their jobs.

Both these approaches arise from a belief that effective change can only be made through expert appraisal of how things are done. Managers and consultants are brought in and then the change is 'sold' (Rational-Empirical) or 'told' (Power-Coercive) to the people who have to make it work. This approach goes against all that we have learned about how best to lead people, not involving them, not trusting their ability to make a positive contribution, and assuming that having authority (positional power) is enough to get people to do what you want. However, as we have been learning all the way through *Introducing Leadership*, if the people affected by the change are fully involved in the change, it is likely to be a better designed system and they are likely to be more open to the change. This means following a third style of change management:

3 The *Normative-Re-educative* style acknowledges that people are social beings and that they care about their *roles* (what they do in the organization), their *relationships* (whom they work with and how they work together) and the *culture of the organization* or their part of it (the norms and values which guide them, and the significance of symbols and behaviours which demonstrate their status and power).

Leaders do not have to be told that these things matter; for them the Normative-Re-educative approach is the obvious way to go. If people are involved from the beginning, they own the change, it is most likely to work and can be introduced most easily. So why do managers choose the Rational-Empirical or Power-Coercive approach? Because they do not trust the people affected by the change, because it means being open and discussing the external pressures which makes them fearful they will lose authority (they do not control the world outside), and it means they have to spend a lot of time explaining things they may not fully understand themselves. In other words, it reflects their lack of confidence in themselves. Leaders are open about what is happening, have the confidence to admit what they do not know and are willing to listen to anyone else who may know – they trust the people they lead.

Learning from Kurt Lewin

Kurt Lewin (who died in 1947) was a German psychologist who pioneered research into group dynamics (how people in groups interact with each other) and organizational development (how organizations change). His contribution to our understanding of organizations is immense; Lewin emphasized the importance of people in the change process and he offered two particular insights into this process:

- force field analysis
- unfreeze–change–refreeze model of change.

Force field analysis is a technique for assessing how likely it is that change will occur. It is based on the concept of forces for and against change, primarily the perceptions of people in the organization about a particular force, and its influence. Lewin argued that there are two types of forces:

- *Driving forces* that are attempting to push in a particular direction and either initiate change or keep it going
- *Restraining forces*, which act to restrain or reduce the effect of the driving forces.

When the driving forces (encouraging change) equal the pressure of the restraining forces (holding it back), there is equilibrium (no change is possible). However, according to Lewin, simply increasing the driving forces will not bring about change. Instead, it causes the resisting forces to increase (people will resist change) and the current equilibrium is maintained but is put under increased tension, so people feel stressed and are increasingly negative about the change. Instead of increasing the driving forces, the pressures for change, the resisting forces need to be reduced. This allows movement towards the goal and does not increase the tension.

Lewin also suggested that the resistance to change comes particularly from group *norms*, which are part of the culture or sub-culture of the organization (a sub-culture is the specific culture of part of the organization). This culture is reflected in the ways of working that people establish, which become important parts of their relationships with each other. But it also uses symbols and these symbols can be very important – think how much time is spent arguing about who has a reserved car parking space and who does not, the size of someone's desk or who has the 'best' position in the office or workshop.

Key idea

> **Norms**
>
> Norms are the accepted way of doing things, the set of unwritten and unspoken rules that govern how people behave. Most social groups have these rules – you only have to go abroad to find how hard it is to make sense of behaviour that everyone else takes for granted.
>
> Norms exist in all organizations, and in groups in that organization. Two different groups may have very different norms yet are supposedly doing the same thing. Norms are enforced by social pressure; people who break the rules will be pressured by the group, often through non-verbal communication, to adjust their behaviour and bring it into line with what is expected. Where these rules conflict with the organization's rules, it is often the group norms that have precedence. Managers and leaders cannot enforce the rules all the time, but the group can.
>
> You cannot change people's behaviour unless you understand the norms that govern that behaviour. One of the ways to change norms is to break up the social group that enforces them, but you need to be sure that the new groups you form do not carry forward the norms of their earlier groups. That is what the 'storming' and 'norming' phases that Tuckman described are all about, working out which norms to carry forward as well as which new ones to establish.

The second part of Lewin's model of change suggests that, to make change happen, the restraining forces (the pressures to stay the same) have to be removed. He describes this as a three-stage process:

1 *Unfreezing* – explore the driving and restraining forces for change, involving people in this analysis so that they understand

what is happening and can review and revise their own values and expectations from their work roles.

2 *Change* – redesign the work processes in ways that respond to the driving forces *and* the restraining forces, not by ignoring them and assuming that they will be overcome simply by pushing through the change.

3 *Refreeze* – help to establish and support new group norms that will support the new ways of working.

This model (unfreeze – change – refreeze) has been criticized because it ignores the way that organizations are constantly changing these days. However, when contemplating a major change, the sort of change that BPR encourages, it is a useful set of guidelines to help you plan your change programme.

Overcoming barriers to change

Lewin suggests that the resistance to change, the restraining forces, often increases in line with the driving forces, so that the harder you push for change the greater the resistance. Although group norms were picked out especially by Lewin, there are other sources of resistance, creating barriers to change, from the organization's own structures, systems and resources, from individuals who fear change, the loss of status and power, and who lack the ability to adopt new ways of working, and from a lack of leadership.

- *Organizational structures*

  Organizational barriers arise because the organization seems incapable of responding effectively to the proposed change. Structural barriers arise because the organization is designed to work best in the old way, not the new. There is a saying 'structure follows strategy' which means that an organization should be able to change itself to reflect what it wants to do now and in the future, not what it used to do. If the responsibility for a particular activity is spread across different departments it will be done far less effectively than if it were located in one. Structures should be designed to enable the organization to function effectively, not to give power and prestige to those who manage them.

- *Organizational systems and resources*

  Systems are the way that things are done – how resources are organized to enable a process to occur. If the system is designed to deliver something else, then it will continue to be better at doing that than doing what is needed now. Resources are essential if change is to be introduced. That means giving the change team access to the resources they need to make the change work. If the change team lacks resources it is undermined because it clearly lacks support. The lack of resources will often be used as a bargaining ploy by those who control the resources to ensure that the change goes the way that they want, rather than what is best for the organization.

- *Individual willingness to change*

  Individual barriers arise because people have their own goals and their own strengths and weaknesses. Change leaders need to understand how individuals think and react if they are to persuade them to change. It is important not to make rash judgements about people's willingness to change – just because a group of people have worked here a long time or always done it one way does not mean they will not change – they may never have been given the chance. Equally, people who are new, young and not used to the way that things are done may prove surprisingly resistant to new ideas – they came here because of how things are done now, not how they are being changed.

- *Individual fear of change*

  Fear of change is the greatest barrier with many people – they prefer the 'devil they know'. This is not unreasonable – change brings uncertainty and can be personally threatening. Some people lack confidence in their ability to meet new people and do new things, so change undermines their confidence further. There may have been other changes that have been problematic, so they have every reason to believe that this one will be too – experience tells them it does not work and just makes life difficult. By involving people in the change process, allowing them to move at a pace which is comfortable and offering them the chance to take some control over the process, then these fears may be lessened.

- *Individual fear of loss of status and power*

  Many people fear a loss of status and power from change, especially managers whose areas of responsibility are being changed by somebody else. They will resist the change, even undermine it if they can, to retain their power and control. This is not surprising since status and power are often more important than financial rewards – the less people have, the more they value it for what it brings to them. Change can threaten this in two ways, by the change leader taking over responsibility for how they and their people do things, and by reducing their future status and power in any new way of working. Change leaders need to involve people in the change process to give them a sense of influence, keep them informed about what is going on, and consult them on issues that directly affect them. If they still resist, then change leaders need sanctions to force through the change, which means that there must be support from the top.

- *Individual abilities*

  Many people are not sure they are capable of adopting new ways of working and so they resist change to avoid the challenge. Training is one part of the process of overcoming such worries, but it needs to be timed carefully. Do it too early and people have forgotten what they learned by the time new systems are in place. Do it too late and fear will have created barriers or, worse, people will start doing the tasks wrong, and will then be able to say, 'I told you so', when things go wrong. Training is best if it can be made available 'on demand', supplemented by workplace coaching, to help people put what they have learned into practice straightaway.

- *Lack of leadership*

  The biggest barrier of all is a lack of leadership in taking on new roles. If people are not well led and supported they will feel uncertain about what is expected of them and how they are supposed to respond to the change. However, it can be difficult for a change leader if the organization itself lacks effective leadership. If this is the case, as a change leader, you will need to consider how it will affect the ability of the change team to make the change happen, and set your goals accordingly.

Whatever barriers you face, be alert to them, do not ignore them and build into your plans ways to address them as early as possible.

Working with a change team

A change leader should not try to make change happen alone. Effective change depends upon a team approach, as this allows different points of view, multiple skills and shared responsibility for making the process happen. A good change leader will build a team and will draw on the talents of all the team to make change happen. A change team is more than simply a group of helpers, it means having:

- An *agreed purpose* – the team needs a clear focus and objectives, so that change addresses the real drivers for change
- *Shared responsibility* – all team members must accept responsibility for these common goals, with individual goals to help achieve these common goals
- *Organization* – the team must have some sense of structure and roles, so that everyone understands what everyone else is doing
- *Trust and support* – team members must trust each other to achieve what they are working towards and, in return, be prepared to help and support each other to achieve these goals.

The practicalities of organizing a change team include ensuring that the team's members all have clear:

1 *roles and responsibilities* – who does what
2 *authority* – what each one can decide on their own, what the team as a whole can decide, and what has to be referred to others to decide
3 *accountability* – to whom individuals and the team as a whole are responsible, and for what.

The same is true for you, as a change leader. You must:

1 have a clear *brief or terms of reference* – so you know what is expected of you
2 know what *power* you have – do you control the budget entirely or must you get approval for expenditure above certain levels, or must it all be approved by a line manager?
3 know to whom you are *accountable* and how you are expected to account for your actions
4 have effective, open *communication* with your team and the people involved in or affected by the change.

Communication, especially, is vital to a successful change team, as team members need to know what each other is doing and how the team is progressing. It is also vital in keeping those affected by the change informed about the direction and progress of change. Finally, it is important to keep the stakeholders – the decision-makers, gatekeepers and sponsors – informed about progress, to maintain the coalition of support for the change, and is a key part of accountability. Communication should not be an after-thought; get it planned and organized right at the start of the change process by asking yourself:

- Who needs to be kept informed (distinguishing different categories of people having different communication needs)?
- When they need to be kept informed (how often and at particular times)?
- How best to inform them (verbal briefings, formal reports, etc.)?
- What to inform them about (because different people will need to know different things)?

Above all else, remember why people are being kept informed. Different people need to know different things because they have different interests – decision-makers will be very interested in budgetary updates, those affected by the change will want to know about disruptions to their working environment, etc. Team members might be happy with weekly e-mails with bullet-point updates, sponsors may want a formal report, because for team members it is just a way of keeping up to date with each other, whereas for sponsors it is evidence that they made the right decision to back the project.

Being a change leader is all about using those skills and abilities that we looked at in detail at the beginning of *Introducing Leadership*:

- Having good communication and social skills
- Being dependable, conscientious and honest, and showing integrity
- Being innovative and having a vision of where you are heading
- Having personal drive, a sense of purpose, motivation and emotional maturity
- Having the self-confidence to accept a challenge and the risks associated with it
- Motivating others to achieve agreed goals
- Inspiring trust in others.

These skills ensure that people are kept informed and are listened to, that change teams are kept focused on the goals of the exercise and that, as a change leader, you are able to manage yourself (using your time wisely and not being diverted from your priorities).

Above all, you will have the respect of others and so will be better able to persuade people of the value of the change.

Alongside this, as a change leader, remember to keep developing yourself, by monitoring and reviewing the progress of the change project and reflecting on your own performance. By doing this you can learn from experience and improve your own performance and the performance of the team you are leading. You need to be open to feedback from your team and your manager, recognizing that the way that others see you affects their willingness to follow your lead. Above all, you need to remember that, as a change leader, you are first and foremost, a leader of people, and that your success as a leader can only be measured by their willingness to follow.

Summary

- The pace of change in modern society is continuing to grow, putting pressure on organizations to respond or suffer the consequences. Effective leaders are alert to the pressures for change on their organizations and its readiness and ability to respond to them.

- One approach to change is Business Process Re-engineering, which asks the question, 'If the organization did not exist today, how would we create it?' It involves bringing all the tasks associated with producing a product or supplying a service into a single integrated process, from the beginning to the end.

- Being a change leader means bringing people with you, involving them throughout the change process (a Normative-Re-educative style) to develop their roles, relationships and the organizational culture.

- Change leaders should be aware of the restraining forces that counteract the driving forces for change, and deal with them, rather than simply increase the pressure for change. A major source of resistance to change are the organizational norms, the unofficial rules that govern people's behaviour, and it is these, in particular, that the Normative-Re-educative style seeks to modify.

- Change leaders also need to be alert to organizational and individual barriers to change but, above all else, to any lack of leadership from elsewhere and make sure that, as leaders of change teams, they make the most of the opportunities available.

- Both change team members and change team leaders need clear roles, responsibilities and a sense of accountability, supported by open communications, and the leader also needs to possess all those skills and abilities that *Introducing Leadership* has identified as the key to effective leadership.

Notes

1 Michael Hammer and James Champy's *Re-engineering the Corporation: A manifesto for business revolution* was published by HarperBusiness in 1993.
2 The second edition was published in 1999 by Capstone. Diane Coyle now runs a consultancy that specializes in advising organizations on how to cope with the effects of the changes that she described in *The Weightless World*.
3 In 1999, a transatlantic cable was laid containing eight fibres, each with 120 gigabits per second capacity, able to handle 15 million calls simultaneously.
4 The MSC Pamela, launched in 2005, is 321 metres long, weighs more than 100 000 tonnes and has a maximum capacity of 9200 TEU – 'twenty foot equivalent units' – according to Wikipedia.

Appendix What level of leader/manager are you?

The three levels of leader/manager described here (team leader, first line and middle manager) are based on definitions developed by the Institute of Leadership and Management, and used with their permission.

Are you a 'Team Leader'?

1 You regard yourself as being part of the team you lead.

2 You mainly spend your time in similar types of tasks as your fellow team members.

3 Being a team leader is an additional responsibility to these tasks.

4 You have to plan for activities over the next few days or weeks, but not for longer periods.

5 You are responsible for the day-to-day performance of the team's tasks.

6 You allocate tasks (or ensure tasks are agreed) between team members.

7 You help individual team members to perform their jobs (e.g. by coaching them or just giving them advice or guidance).

8 You are responsible to your manager for ensuring that all the tasks required are performed to the right level of quality and to look for ways for improving quality.

9 You act as the main communication channel between the team and your managers.

10 You are responsible for watching out for changes in customers' or supplier requirements, or for any special requirements, and advising your line manager.

11 Customers' or suppliers' complaints or problems are passed to you by members of your team if they cannot easily deal with them.

12 You have to consult your line manager before you make any significant changes in the way that the team operates.

13 Because of your experience or technical competence, you are expected by team members to be able to deal with operational problems that arise.

Are you a 'First Line Manager'?

1 Being a first line manager (team leader, supervisor, etc.) is your primary or most important job, although you may also do the same work as team members.

2 You and/or your team and/or your line manager regard you as being slightly apart from the team you lead.

3 You spend only part of your time in similar types of tasks as the rest of the team.

4 You ensure that tasks are allocated to team members.

5 You are responsible for ensuring that team members are competent to do the tasks allocated to them, and for identifying any training and development needs they may have.

6 You are expected to make decisions (within limits) that may have a limited impact on the organization's costs, such as agreeing or recommending overtime or new suppliers.

7 You get involved in planning activities for the next few months, but rarely for periods beyond a year ahead.

8 If you were concerned about an employee's behaviour or performance, you would formally warn the person, and notify your line manager.

9 You get asked to advise on decisions in relation to appointments of new team members.

10 You feel you have some (possibly limited) autonomy or freedom to make decisions about how your team works.

11 You are responsible for advising on quality standards, ensuring that quality standards are met and leading team members in seeking ways to improve quality.

12 You are expected (by team members and/or your line manager) to be aware of (or find out about) developments going on within the organization that may affect your team's activities in the longer term.

13 You are expected to be able to recognize or resolve many straightforward operational problems, because of your experience or technical competence, and to deal with most problems that arise with customers or suppliers.

14 You are expected to be able to judge whether or not your manager needs to be informed about operational, customer or supplier problems, or whether you are able to resolve them yourself.

15 You sometimes get asked to join project teams, or work with such teams, to make changes in your area of activity.

16 You are consulted about budgets, but decisions about them are kept largely in the hands of your line manager.

17 You are given only limited control over a budget for your area of activity, on which you have to report regularly.

Are you a 'Middle Manager'?

1 Being a manager is your primary or most important job.

2 Your role as a manager clearly distinguishes you from those you manage.

3 Any work you do, apart from your specifically managerial role, is to do with a specialist technical, professional or similar responsibility.

4 You have team leaders or first line managers (supervisors, etc.) in charge of teams or other groups reporting to you.

5 You are accountable to senior managers for the performance of those who report to you.

6 You are responsible for ensuring that team members are competent in their job roles, and for ensuring that any training and development needs they may have are being met.

7 You are responsible for managing a budget and making decisions that have an impact on the organization's costs, and/or revenues within the overall constraints of the agreed budget.

8 You are expected to play an active part in planning activities for periods of a year or more ahead.

9 You are expected to take responsibility for ensuring that employees perform their roles competently, abide by the rules and procedures of the organization and, if necessary, with

appropriate professional advice, to instigate disciplinary or competence proceedings.

10 You negotiate with external suppliers and customers, to agree prices, specifications, delivery and other contract terms.

11 You have responsibility for ensuring that a range of resources (people, equipment, buildings, etc.) is used effectively, and to make recommendations for future investment in resources and/or a revised pattern of resource utilization.

12 You are responsible for ensuring that standards of quality are set and/or raised, and that performance is monitored and improved.

13 You decide (perhaps with others) on appointments of new employees.

14 You feel you have a fair degree of autonomy or freedom to make decisions about how the people you manage should work, to make changes to systems and procedures.

15 You are expected to be aware of developments going on within the organization and to be consulted about any that may affect the activities of those you manage.

16 You occasionally become involved in projects to make significant changes to activities, possibly in a project leadership role.

17 You are expected to ensure that operational problems are resolved and to deal personally with more significant problems that arise with important customers and suppliers.

18 You are expected to advise senior managers only of those problems that are particularly significant, in terms of cost or the future market or supply situation.

19 You have control over and are accountable for, a budget for your area of activity, possibly with some freedom to reallocate funds between different budget areas.

Index

INDEX

243